THE
SOCIAL
ASSOCIATION

5 key skills not-for-profits need
to increase member engagement,
generate ROI and create a thriving
online community.

MEL KETTLE

www.melkettle.com

"Social media is now an essential component of non-profit community engagement. Mel Kettle, a real-world communicator herself who has pioneered how social media builds non-profit brands, provides both a strategic overview and a tactical blueprint to exactly what you need to know for success in the digital world. This is no academic tome, it is practical and useful advice you can apply to grow your organisation today."

– David Meerman Scott, marketing strategist, entrepreneur and best-selling author of 10 books, including _The New Rules of Marketing & PR_ – now available in 29 languages from Albanian to Vietnamese

"The old models of engaging members in associations have changed. Previously, it was about events, publications and direct mail. Today, members want more just-in-time meaning and connection with their industry. The balance of value add against return on investment of social media is constant. Mel's book shows the future of member engagement and simplifies the complexities of social media for associations. As a result of following her five steps, they create connected communities of tomorrow's industry leaders."

– Jane Anderson, authentic leadership expert, certified speaker, award-winning blogger and author of five books

"Today's member organisation CEOs need to ensure their communications drives member value and this book is a must read for the entire team. We are no longer in an age where information slowly filters out. Communication needs to be strategic, tailored to suit our members, funders and stakeholders, it needs to be timely, concise, easy to understand and we all need to measure our organisations' communication success through analytics. Enjoy this book and share it around!"

– Kris Trott, Chief Executive Officer, Queensland Alliance for Mental Health

"This book is a practical guide for getting started or getting better with your social media strategies. Whether you love it or loathe it, social media can be used to strengthen conversations, connections and community. As a social media strategist with a strong professional commitment to supporting associations, Mel shows us what we need to do to do it well."
– **Kathryn Woods, General Manager, Children's Services, The Creche and Kindergarten Association Ltd**

"Social media for any NFP is as essential as the vision it works to. It doesn't have to be excessive, but it does have to exist because online is where anyone and everyone is going to get all the information about YOU! A well-thought-out strategy and some creativity will determine how successful you will be in reaching your audiences, potential supporters, untapped donors and future members about who you are, what you do and how amazing your work is. First step in building your online presence is to read *The Social Association*. Mel Kettle has put together the 'bible of social media', especially for NFPs that may be time poor but need to be noticed."
– **Dr Anita Heiss, author and Manager, Epic Good Foundation**

"Mel Kettle is one of Australia's top social media marketing and communication experts. Mel's style is clear, easy to understand and she holds nothing back to make sure you understand what you need to know to use social networks in your association. She does an excellent job of sharing statistics and relatable case studies of other organisations using social media. This book is dripping with insight and experience gathered from Mel's passion for lifelong learning. It will push your association to sensible and innovative communication and connectivity heights with your members."
– **Heather Smith, chartered accountant, cloud solutions expert, business automation virtuoso, YouTuber, podcaster, author, speaker**

"The secret to attracting and retaining association members is engagement. This engagement is usually done by providing value, creating social interaction and by sharing experience within the association's realm of expertise. Social media is a key tool to easily and affordably achieve this. As Mel points out in her book, there are some key stumbling blocks and key elements to making social media work for associations. Mel's straightforward, no-nonsense approach to social media for associations is fantastic. It makes achieving success in this important part of our association's future so much more possible. I highly recommend this book and engaging Mel to assist you in getting it right the first time."
– Warwick Merry CSP, 2017 President, Professional Speakers Australia

"Mel Kettle knows social media. In her book, *The Social Association*, she gives practical, no-nonsense advice specifically designed to help not-for-profit groups navigate the sometimes daunting social media scene. From my experience as a board director in not-for-profits, I understand that engaging effectively with members and other stakeholders is critically important. *The Social Association* is well-researched, easy to read and steps you through the key skills needed to add value to your members through these low-cost and accessible platforms. If you're aiming to grow your membership, this is the book you need."
– Dr Monique Beedles, author, speaker and experienced board director

"This is the only book associations need to start or to ramp up their social media with confidence and structure. It's the rule book for social networking and engaging current and potential members, sponsors and donors. Mel has taken the guess work out and added the structure, permission and insight when it comes to social media for associations."
– Sally Foley-Lewis, productive leadership speaker, author and mentor

"Social media is very important for any association. Mel Kettle is a true expert and describes how to communicate and use social media effectively in a highly practical way. This is the perfect guide on how to move away from reliance on emails (where members complain about being 'spammed'). Using Mel's great advice, any association can effectively communicate and engage with members and prospects using social media. I have known Mel professionally and on social media for many years – she is a total professional and highly engaging.
#melknowshershitandistotallyawesome."
– Mark Woodrow, President, International Association of Business Communicators (NSW) 2016, 2017; Client Success Manager, iSentia

"Whether you are social media savvy or a complete novice, Mel's book provides solid and practical steps to help you on your social media journey. Mel provides a compelling argument for social media in a helpful, trusted and non-preachy way. A highly recommended read for anyone embarking on a social media strategy and wanting to connect and engage authentically with their members and community."
– Sarah Smith, Director, Media and Communication Services and experienced board director

"We, as association professionals, complain about and compare our reducing membership numbers and retention rates. Mel provides us with a clear understanding of social media, why we must be involved and steps to ensure our associations have successful strategies and execution.
#membersarepeople #associationsarecommunities #readmelsbook."
– Glen Harriss, State Manager – Queensland, Sports Medicine Australia

"A book which makes me feel young again! Now I understand what all this social media is about and how we can use it best for our association. Mel Kettle has made it easy to understand what we should really do to make social media work for us, make it worth the effort, and not get caught out!"
– Richard Stokes, Executive Director, Australian Boarding Schools Association

For Mum and Dad.
You always supported me, although I'm sure there were many times you wondered, "What exactly is she thinking?"
I miss you. xx

ABOUT THE AUTHOR

Mel Kettle is a communication specialist who is determined to demystify social media. Mel helps associations, not-for-profits, business leaders and boards clearly understand how social media can be used to help them achieve their organisational goals.

With more than 20 years' professional experience (as well as a Master of Business and Master of Public Health), Mel has found one of the biggest challenges organisations face is how to communicate effectively so they can attract, retain and engage customers. She provides tailored and practical communication solutions to achieve this, through mentoring, training, consulting and speaking.

Mel's clients include associations, research centres, charities, government and businesses. She has been a board member for the International Association of Business Communicators (Qld) and The Queensland Choir, and has been on the Management Committee of War Child Australia.

An accomplished and sought-after speaker on communication and social media, Mel delivers presentations that are packed with relevant examples, real-world thinking and practical advice.

In her spare time, Mel cooks, giggles at the antics of her backyard chickens and reads crime thrillers.

The Social Association is Mel's first book.

To find out more about Mel and her programs, go to www.melkettle.com.

MEL KETTLE

ACKNOWLEDGEMENTS

Over the years, I have attended countless book launches for many of my clever and talented friends. It was at one of these about 10 years ago when author Nick Earls said to me, while signing his latest book, "When will we be here for your book launch?" I recall muttering something along the lines of, "Maybe one day ...," then fleeing before he could pin me down to a topic and a date. Well, Nick, here you are.

I first had the idea for this book about a year ago. I was working with quite a few associations and member organisations. When looking for resources for them to read, I realised there was nothing on social media specifically for them. So, I decided to write something.

I have many people to thank for helping me along the way:

- Gail and Stuart Fowler, who met me at the Hotel Vancouver in 1995 and immediately offered me a job. Gail, your confidence in me will never be forgotten.

- Belinda and Julian Moore, who reminded me just how much I love working with associations.

- Carole Green, Keith Hampson and Peter Scuderi, my first clients when I started consulting, and who frequently and consistently gave me work and many referrals during those early years.

- All the clients I have worked with over the past 11 years.

- Everyone who generously shared their experiences and expertise – some of you I have mentioned throughout.

- To Matt Church, Peter Cook, Col Fink and many others at Thought Leaders Business School, you gave me a clear process to get my knowledge down on paper. I suspect this book would still be in my head were it not for your guidance and support. And pink sheets. Let's not forget the pink sheets.

- My friends and family in Brisbane, around Australia and around the world – to list you all would take pages and pages. You have been there quietly (some less quietly ...) in the background, but always there for a chat, a meal, a wine and often a bed. Which isn't related to the wine. In case you're wondering. Thank you especially to Jules, Em, Sam and Zoe Kettle, Jo Bargon, Collette Barton-Ross, Aisha Barton-Ross, Samantha Ford, Jan Moore, Susan Lambe, Pat Reid, Gerry and Lynne Bissett, Jen Dainer, Sally Bagshaw, Angela McDonald, Sharon Light, Heather Smith, Alisha Lynch, Kerri Rodley, Kirsten Binnie, Fiona Home, Anita Heiss, Dyan Johnson, Kylie Meller, Pam and Bob Turner, and the others I've not mentioned, for your love and support.

- To my friends and colleagues who helped get this book out. You shared stories, gave me support and love, and proofread pages of my book when I was reading the same sentence over and over and over. Thank you especially to Sally Foley-Lewis, Emily Verstege, Kate Billing, my editor Lauren Shay and publisher Sylvie Blair.

- To the many, many café owners and staff who have allowed me to sit quietly and work, and who have kept me fuelled with caffeine. Thank you.

- Thank you to my mentor Jane Anderson, who has guided me through this book writing gig with patience and kindness.

Finally, thank you to Shaun. You might roll your eyes when I say, "I've been thinking...", but your unwavering love and support through sickness and through health, through sadness and through joy have meant more than a piece of paper ever could. I love you.

MEL KETTLE

FOREWORD

The operating landscape for member-based associations has shifted dramatically in the past 10 years. The advent of significant technological innovation has driven massive changes in the way we communicate.

While these new communication channels provide many opportunities and advantages for associations, it has also made it relatively easy for others to compete against the products, services communications and events of most associations.

In this new environment, a key competitive advantage for many associations is having a strong community. Strong associations have discovered that an emotionally engaged stakeholder group is exceptionally difficult for others to compete with. Associations that can successfully nurture this community are emerging through the changes to their operating environment more powerfully than ever before.

Associations must strive to become facilitators of meaningful engagements if they wish to generate tangible outcomes for their members. Social media provides a powerful way to achieve this and for it to be a significantly successful element, it must be used strategically, as part of an integrated communications plan.

Many of us know this instinctively. It seems obvious. However, many associations find social media to be a drain on time and resources with little return.

There are many reasons for this. Many don't understand the reason why they use social media or why they use special channels. They don't apply appropriate tools to measure success or (worst of all) don't have any way of measuring the effectiveness of their social media efforts.

Social media is no longer optional. The generation now entering the workforce, Generation Z (born after 1996), is also called the Snapchat Generation. They are social media savvy and have never known a non-connected world. For many of this generation (and many younger Generation Ys), if you are not on social media then you don't exist.

By 2029, most association boards, members and staff will be Generation X or younger. Associations seeking to position themselves for strong growth into the future must ensure they excel in this critical communication tool.

Taking the time to set up your social strategy right will reap significant rewards. And the book that you hold in your hands is a strong step towards this.

Mel Kettle is Australasia's foremost specialist in social media for associations. With more than 20 years' experience in this field, she brings a wealth of practical insights and advice. Her programs and guidance will enable your association to begin building a powerful online community that will assist you to better achieve your organisational goals.

Good luck … and I look forward to seeing you online.

Warm regards,

Belinda Moore
Strategic Membership Solutions
@membershipgeek

CONTENTS

INTRODUCTION

Social media. Why is it so important? What difference can it make? When do we need to use it? How do we start?

Social media is a communication tool that helps us better get to know the people who do business with us. It allows us to ask and answer questions. It allows us to listen and observe. It allows us to have conversations, build relationships and engage with people. It allows people to get to know, like and trust us.

I have been active on social media since 2007, blogging since 2008 and dabbling with podcasts since 2015. The people I have conversed with, engaged with and built relationships with have kindly, generously and often unknowingly provided me with countless personal and professional opportunities, enhanced my knowledge, given me courage to try new (and often scary-to-me) things, comforted me, and shared my joy, my anger, my sadness and my grief.

I'll never forget the day I realised the power of social media to provide personal love and comfort. It was August 2010. I had been an active user of Twitter for about 18 months. I loved the conversations, the people I met online, the knowledge I gained from the information shared. For much of that time, I tweeted about anything and everything that interested me. Food, travel, books, TV, movies, a bit about marketing and public speaking. I had many, many conversations with people, most of whom I had not met and probably never will meet.

On 22 August, I tweeted that my mother unexpectedly died. What happened next touched me in a way I couldn't anticipate. Hundreds of people – again, most of whom I had never met – tweeted me love, condolences and offers of support. It was overwhelming yet very comforting. This support from strangers (as well as from many friends) helped me in ways I still struggle to articulate.

A few months later, in January 2011, much of Queensland, including Brisbane where I live, flooded. I saw a tweet about taking food to volunteers to provide some #bakedrelief and thought, "What a good idea." My kitchen became a hotbed of activity as I baked and tweeted incessantly over the next few days, little realising a social movement had been born.

#bakedrelief symbolised what can happen when the power of social media comes into play. Within 48 hours of the first use of that hashtag, thanks to the reach and influence generated by Twitter, and to a lesser extent Facebook and blogs, help was crowdsourced in real-time. Over the following weeks, thousands of people donated money, time and food to help those in need. Would this help have been given without social media? Yes, of course it would have. Would it have happened with the same speed and volume? Most definitely not.

These two experiences helped shape my view of how social media provides the opportunity for people to get to know, like and trust each other.

I have been involved with associations and member-based organisations since I was at university in the late '80s and a member of student organisations. In the years since, I have worked as a professional conference organiser, coordinating events for medical, legal and engineering associations. Peak industry bodies were stakeholders I negotiated with when I worked for the Queensland Government and with cooperative research centres. I have been a member, sat on boards, spoken at conferences and worked closely with many associations as they endeavoured to provide a better experience for their members.

Throughout this book, I have used the word "association". This is intended to capture the broad range of member organisations, both non- and for-profit, that include professional associations, industry associations, charities, trade unions, sporting clubs, loyalty programs, churches, insurance providers, credit unions, managed-fund providers, community organisations, chambers of commerce, service clubs, cultural institutions and political parties.

The world is changing at a rapid rate. However, take comfort in this: people do business with people they know, like and trust. This is human nature and will not change, regardless of demographic, cultural, social and economic trends. Your success will be, in part, determined by how you demonstrate your value. Yes, technology is changing how we do business, but inherently people need to feel valued, needed and wanted. Social media can help you achieve this.

I'm excited to share this book with you. Whether you are the CEO of a professional body with 20,000 members or the president of your Neighbourhood Watch, if you want to learn how to effectively use social media to create an engaged community, then this book is for you.

This book explores the five key skills you need to increase member engagement, generate a return on investment and create a thriving online community. Each chapter has practical advice, real-world examples and questions for you to consider.

If you have questions, you can find me on Facebook (www.facebook.com/MelKettleBiz), LinkedIn (www.linkedin.com/in/melkettle) and, of course, on Twitter (@melkettle). I look forward to talking to you.

Mel x

MEL KETTLE

CHAPTER 1

SOCIAL MEDIA AND ASSOCIATIONS

"We don't have a choice on whether we do social media, the question is how well we do it."
– Erik Qualman

The world has changed how it communicates, and too many associations haven't kept up. Social media is becoming an increasingly important and non-negotiable way to communicate with members and stakeholders.

The traditional communication model – where associations decide what they want to tell their members, write something, then distribute it via their magazines and newsletters – is now largely irrelevant.

Today, communication is two-way. Your members want to be able to engage with you via Facebook, Twitter, LinkedIn and Instagram, as well as via email, messaging apps and phone. They want to read your blog, watch your videos and listen to your podcasts.

Social media, and technology more broadly, is more affordable than ever. Social media is free to use! Yes, you need to pay people to manage it (as you must do for all communication channels) and there are many paid tools you can use to make it quicker and easier, but the actual technology itself is free.

Yet too many associations are either not using it at all or using it poorly – and in ways that discourage engagement from their members.

As American entrepreneur and best-selling author Gary Vaynerchuk tells us, "If you don't adjust to the reality of a situation, you will be left behind." I couldn't agree more.[1]

While it may seem that a shiny, new social media channel or technology emerges every second week, when it comes to human behaviour, little has changed. People still do business with people they know, like and trust. Service excellence and consistency of value remain essential to business success.

We continue to get our news by reading, listening and watching – but what has changed is the way we do these activities. Today, instead of having a newspaper delivered to our door each morning, we read blogs, websites and online news sites on our phones, tablets and computers 24/7. We might still listen to the radio, but we are more likely to listen to a digital station or a podcast.

In terms of video, YouTube, Facebook, Instagram, Snapchat and video-streaming services such as Netflix are rapidly overtaking free-to-air television. Research in 2016 showed that in the 13- to 24-year-old age group, YouTube was the most viewed video

---

1 Kettle, M. "Lessons from @GaryVee", melkettle.com, 9 November, 2017. https://www.melkettle.com/2017/11/lessons-from-garyvee/ (accessed 10 November, 2017).

platform (watched by 85%), followed by Netflix (66%) and television (65%).[2]

WHY ASSOCIATIONS SHOULD USE SOCIAL MEDIA

Social media helps associations STAND OUT. Used wisely, it can help you increase awareness of your organisation, demonstrate the value of membership, attract new members, increase member engagement and retention rates, attract people to your events and create a thriving online community.

It can help you amplify your engagement and create strong relationships, ensuring you have a well-connected community with powerful conversations.

It is important to remember that social media is not about sales. It's about being social. That's why it's not called "sales media". The primary purpose of social media is to facilitate relationships.

Did you know, Twitter was originally set up as a communications system that allowed you to send a text message to one number and it would be broadcast to all your friends?[3] And did you know Facebook was established to make the world more open and connected? In fact, Facebook's mission is to "give people the power to build community and bring the world closer together."[4]

---

2 Spangler, T. "Younger Viewers Watch 2.5 Times More Internet Video Than TV (Study)", *Variety*, 29 March, 2016. http://variety.com/2016/digital/news/millenni-al-gen-z-youtube-netflix-video-social-tv-study-1201740829/ (accessed 10 November, 2017).

3 Carlson, Nicholas. "The Real History of Twitter", *Business Insider*, 14 April, 2011. https://www.businessinsider.com.au/how-twitter-was-founded-2011-4 (accessed 25 October, 2017).

4 Facebook. https://www.facebook.com/pg/facebook/about/ (accessed 25 October, 2017).

I don't see any mention of sales there!

Two of the biggest challenges facing associations today include how to engage members and how to demonstrate the value of membership. Research from the 2017 *Membership Marketing Benchmarking Report*[5] shows that new technology, including social media and online marketing, has helped increase member engagement. Providing members with new products and services that deliver what they want, when they want it, has also created more vibrant memberships. When looking at these products and services, the report reveals that many traditional offerings, such as insurance programs and book or directory purchases, are declining. However, activities such as participating in the public and private social networks of the association, attending webinars, acquiring or maintaining certification to increase professional credentials, and participating in young professionals programs are driving an increase in member engagement.

It's important to demonstrate that your association has a wide range of benefits that extend beyond events and face-to-face networking activities. I recently asked a question on Facebook and LinkedIn to find out why people were a member of an association and the benefits they received. I must say, I was saddened by many of the responses. They clearly demonstrated many associations were doing a poor job of articulating their member benefits. Responses, both positive and negative, included:

> *"I'm not a member of any professional associations anymore. All the benefits/events/training opportunities were held in capital cities and travelling to attend them isn't feasible. So, membership fees were a waste of money as I got zero benefits."*
> *– Lisa*

---

5 Marketing General Incorporated. 2017 *Membership Marketing Benchmarking Report*, 2017. http://www.marketinggeneral.com/ (accessed 25 October, 2017).

"My professional association offered totally crummy benefits and last-century customer experience." – Emily

"I was a member of Drug & Alcohol Nurses of Australasia, but other than a cut price on conferences, it didn't offer much so I dropped out." – Wendy

"I was a founding member of one: Australian Science Communicators. It was invaluable in the early days when 'science communicator' was a fledgling profession, and you were often the lone person in the place with that role. Great networking, mentoring and professional development opportunities. I still maintain an associate membership despite a career change because I still support what they do ... and I like going to the end-of-year quiz night to socialise with former colleagues." – Corinna Lange

"The only reason I am a member is for reduced insurance premiums." – Kate

"I'm a member of the Australian Medical Association. I've heard it said before of associations that you derive value from what you contribute rather than what you get from them, and that is probably true for me. I was president of the Australian Medical Students' Association (AMSA) and I valued it greatly, but that was because I volunteered so much time, rather than for anything I got personally. I suspect I valued it more than a student who wasn't directly involved but joined for membership benefits.

"In terms of engaging members, I find that from the inside looking out, there is often a focus on wanting to 'show people' what you're doing as a means to engage them further. People want to focus on email/social media strategies, etc. But if the first thing I said is true, that doesn't really make sense – you get broader and better engagement (and higher membership) if you are doing more things that people find relevant. The brand

should be relevant to all kinds of different interests. Perhaps that's particularly important in organised medicine since it seems to be a pretty broad church." – Dr James Lawler

Using social media allows us to have conversations, build relationships and create a community. This, in turn, helps us show value in membership. Keep reading to find out how you can do this!

BENEFITS OF USING SOCIAL MEDIA

Social media can help you achieve your membership key performance indicators (KPIs) as it gives you the opportunity to demonstrate the value you provide. By creating and sharing content that educates your audience, you encourage involvement and create a community.

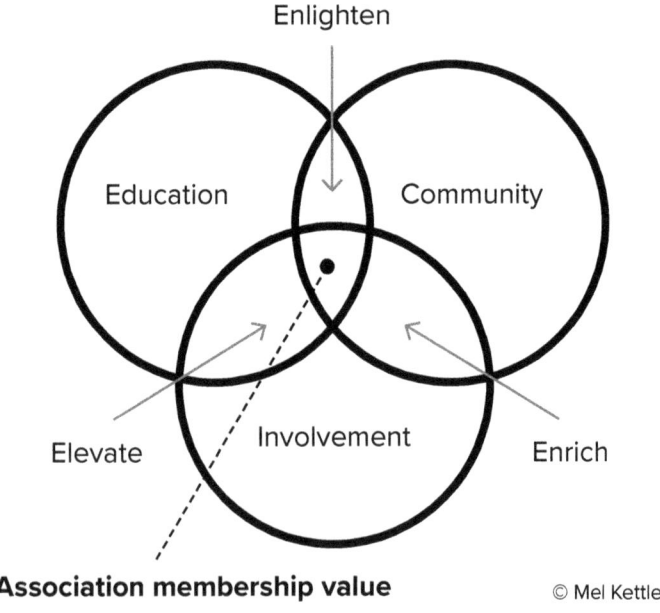

Association membership value   © Mel Kettle

Consider using social media as a low-cost way to educate and enlighten your audience. Use it to share and discuss business ideas. Answer questions and help solve the challenges your members face. Follow your peers, colleagues, influencers and other interesting people from around the world, and share their content with your audience.

By demonstrating the human side of your organisation, you encourage members to get involved. Remember, people do business with people they know, like and trust, so help your members get to know your team. Ask for and give referrals. Perhaps you can't refer specific members, but you can create a member directory you can share with people seeking experts in your industry.

Create a community that enriches the member experience. Talk to your members via your chosen social media channels, and strengthen relationships by engaging in conversations with current and prospective members. Following people you don't know can lead to rewarding business and personal relationships.

The five steps to using social media to help achieve your membership KPIs are:

1. Identify clear goals.

2. Build your social media profile.

3. Develop social media and content strategies that solve your members' problems.

4. Follow your members on social media, have conversations and build relationships with them – this allows them to get to know, like and trust you. Incorporate member social media account details in your member application renewal forms and capture this information in your database.

5. New and renewal member campaigns. If you have taken the time to do steps 1-4, then your members should know how you provide value. This will make it far easier when you reach out to new members or existing members at renewal time, and should lead to a higher return. Make sure your sales scripts include a mention of your social media accounts, and when members have engaged with you.

If you are doing these steps, you should notice an increase in your member renewal rates.

WHY ASSOCIATIONS DON'T USE SOCIAL MEDIA

I speak with a lot of associations, and if they don't use social media, I ask them why. There are five reasons I am repeatedly given:

1. MY MEMBERS AREN'T USING SOCIAL MEDIA

We know this simply isn't true. The *Sensis Social Media Report 2017*[6], an annual survey of consumers and businesses on how they use social networking sites, indicates 84% of Australians access the internet daily and 79% use social media. To break it down further, the report found that social media is almost universally used by the 18-29-year age group (99%), with significant increases in usage over the past 12 months by the 30-39-year age group (up from 82% to 96%) and the 40-49-year age group (up from 70% to 86%). Furthermore, 66% of those aged 50 to 64 years and 47% of those aged 65 years and older use social media.

---

6 Sensis Pty Ltd. *Sensis Social Media Report 2017*, Melbourne, 2017. https://www.sensis.com.au/socialmediareport (accessed 25 October, 2017).

Reasons given for social media use included: following or finding out about brands or businesses, to engage with brands for customer-service reasons, and to research products or services to buy. So, don't tell me your members don't use social media.

2. I DON'T WANT TO MAKE A MISTAKE

I hate to break it to you, but everyone makes mistakes on social media. I sure have! The important part of making a mistake isn't the mistake itself, it's how you manage it and learn from it. Owning your mistakes strengthens your relationships with your audience.

My absolute favourite example of a brand effectively dealing with a social media mistake occurred a few years ago when Gloria Huang (@riaglo) accidentally tweeted: "Ryan found two more 4 bottle packs of Dogfish Head's Midas Touch beer ... when we drink we do it right #gettngslizzerd." She tweeted this from the American Red Cross (@RedCross) Twitter account, instead of her personal account. Huang later apologised, saying, "Rogue tweet frm @RedCross due to my inability to use hootsuite ... I wasn't actually #gettingslizzard but just excited #nowembarrassing."[7]

@riaglo
Gloria Huang

Rogue tweet frm @RedCross due to my inability to use hootsuite... I wasn't actually #gettingslizzard but just excited! #nowembarassing

2 hours ago via HootSuite   ☆ Favorite   ♺ Retweet   ↩ Reply

---

7 Nason, Adam. "Employee sends out errant tweet using @RedCross Twitter account", *BeerPulse*, 16 February, 2011. http://beerpulse.com/2011/02/employee-sends-out-drunk-tweet-using-redcross-twitter-account/ (accessed 25 October, 2017).

> **American Red Cross**
> @RedCross
>
> Ryan found two more 4 bottle packs of Dogfish Head's Midas Touch beer.... when we drink we do it right #gettngslizzerd
>
> HootSuite · 2/15/11 11:24 PM

The Red Cross tweeted shortly after, "We've deleted the rogue tweet but rest assured the Red Cross is sober and we've confiscated the keys."[8]

> **American Red Cross** ⊘
> @RedCross   (Follow) ⌄
>
> We've deleted the rogue tweet but rest assured the Red Cross is sober and we've confiscated the keys.
>
> 3:40 PM - 16 Feb 2011

Wendy Harman, then Director of Social Strategy at the American Red Cross, said of the mistake: "My immediate thought when I saw our mistweet was to address it with an equally unexpected reaction – lighthearted humour and acknowledgement. After all, this wasn't a purposeful message gone wrong and it wasn't about the mission of our organisation. Our Twitter account just tripped on the sidewalk, and instead of throwing a temper

---

8 American Red Cross, Twitter, 15 February, 2011. https://twitter.com/RedCross/status/37748007671832576 (accessed 25 October, 2017).

tantrum about tripping, we acted like any self-aware person would: we dusted ourselves off, looked around to acknowledge the trip with those who caught it, and had a chuckle with them."[9]

It's this reaction that no doubt contributed to the increase in donations to the Red Cross in the immediate aftermath of the rogue tweet. Dogfish Head Brewery and the micro-brew community also encouraged people to donate money to the humanitarian organisation.[10]

Compare this to a Twitter debacle at HMV[11] a few years ago, when a member of the retailer's social media team live-tweeted a mass firing of more than 60 employees. HMV removed the tweets, but a quick Google image search of "HMV Twitter" will show you many, many screenshots. The key lesson here is if you're going to sack your social media team, make sure someone else knows how to manage the accounts, and change the passwords immediately!

It's good practice to change all your social media passwords frequently and to always change them when a member of your social media team leaves, regardless of the circumstances.

3. I DON'T KNOW HOW TO START

Like all new things, social media can seem overwhelming at first. Take the time to lay the foundations and plan your strategy. Start with one channel, ideally the one where most of your

---

9 Harman, Wendy. "The Story Behind Red Cross's Twitter Faux Pas", *Tactical Philanthropy*, 25 February, 2011. http://www.tacticalphilanthropy.com/2011/02/the-story-behind-red-crosss-twitter-faux-pas/ (accessed 25 October, 2017).

10 Harman, Wendy. "Twitter Faux Pas", *Red Cross Chat*, 16 February, 2011. https://redcrosschat.org/2011/02/16/twitter-faux-pas/ (accessed 25 October, 2017).

11 Hardawar, D. "Fired employees hijack HMV's Twitter to livetweet their 'mass execution'", *VentureBeat*, 31 January, 2013. https://venturebeat.com/2013/01/31/fired-employees-hijack-hmv-twitter/ (accessed 10 November, 2017).

members or target market hang out. This is likely to be Facebook or LinkedIn.

Please don't be like the communications manager I met recently, who launched six (yes, six!) social media platforms for his association in one week. That's like starting a new diet and eliminating sugar, caffeine, alcohol, wheat and dairy all at once: it's incredibly difficult and you probably wouldn't last the day! Needless to say, this comms manager wasn't coping all that well when I met him 10 days in. Yes, he was re-evaluating his social strategy!

4. PEOPLE MIGHT SAY BAD THINGS ABOUT US

Guess what? If people want to say bad things about you, they will, whether you use social media or not. Social media provides a forum where you can address issues as they arise, allowing you to reply directly to your members and critics. By focusing on people's perception of your organisation, you can take steps to improve. Negative feedback is extremely valuable, as it gives you an insight into how you can enhance the services you provide, the member experience, your employees and any other part of the organisation that is being criticised.

Having said this, there are occasions when brands and people are attacked by internet trolls.

The Urban Dictionary defines "trolling" as:

> *"Being a prick on the internet because you can. Typically unleashing one or more cynical or sarcastic remarks on an innocent bystander, because it's the internet and, hey, you can."*[12]

---

12 "Trolling", *Urban Dictionary*. https://www.urbandictionary.com/define.php?term=trolling (accessed 10 November, 2017).

Wikipedia defines it as:

> *"Someone who posts inflammatory, extraneous, or off-topic messages in an online community, such as a forum, chat room, or blog, with the primary intent of provoking readers into an emotional response or of otherwise disrupting normal on-topic discussion."*[13]

Personally, I like to call them the scum of the internet!

There are international trolling syndicates that deliberately and systematically try to encourage people to harm themselves. While trolls often start attacking a brand's page, their threats and taunts soon become personally directed towards individuals within the organisation. Journalist Ginger Gorman wrote a chilling account of her meeting with an internet troll who relentlessly bullied victims online[14] – it's well worth a read.

Being trolled is extremely rare, but on the off chance it does happen to your association, there are a few things you can do:

1. Don't feed the trolls. Whatever you do, DO NOT respond. This will inflame them further and it is unlikely you will win.

2. If you do respond (and it can be difficult not to), you will likely make the situation worse. There are two options here – one is to close your social media accounts for a couple of weeks and hope the trolls forget about you, and the other is to keep your social accounts active but stop posting for a week or two.

---

13 "Internet troll", *Wikipedia*. https://en.wikipedia.org/wiki/Internet_troll (accessed 10 November, 2017).

14 Gorman, G. "Staring down internet trolls: My disturbing cat and mouse game", *Sydney Morning Herald*, 17 June, 2017. http://www.smh.com.au/lifestyle/news-and-views/news-features/staring-down-internet-trolls-my-disturbing-cat-and-mouse-game-20170616-gwsmld.html (accessed 10 November, 2017).

3. If the trolling becomes particularly inflamed, consider calling upon the expertise of a public relations firm that specialises in online crisis communication.

One of my favourite responses to internet trolls was by Brisbane independent bookstore Avid Reader.[15] It had shared a Facebook post by feminist writer Clementine Ford, and a few hours later was bombarded with one-star reviews by men's rights activists (one of my favourites was: "too outrageous and politically motivated. a place people go to for knowledge, I wouldn't trust this shop for balanced reading."). The store responded to the trolls with humour; however, the real gold appeared when its community leapt to its defence, leaving almost 4,000 five-star reviews in response to the 400-odd one-star reviews.

This response highlights the power of an online community when you take the time to build strong relationships and truly engage with them.

5. TOO RESOURCE INTENSIVE

It's true, social media can be resource intensive. Although it is free to use Facebook, Twitter, LinkedIn, etc., there is a cost in terms of time and salaries for your team.

The key to successfully using social media is knowing where your audience is. Don't spend time on channels where your members and potential members don't play. Take the time to get to know your members and where they hang out. Develop a social media strategy and a detailed content schedule that will help you more effectively serve your members – and save you time.

---

15 Avid Reader Bookshop Facebook page. https://www.facebook.com/pg/avidreader-bookshop/reviews/?ref=page_internal (accessed 10 November, 2017).

There is also a multitude of time-saving tools available. I will talk more about these in Chapter 5.

HOW SOCIAL MEDIA CAN INCREASE MEMBER ENGAGEMENT

"Content is king but engagement is queen,
and the lady rules the house."
– Mari Smith

I'm often asked how associations can better use social media to engage with members, and, in turn, increase word-of-mouth marketing and member retention. I usually remind the asker that people do business with people they know, like and trust. Yes, I say this a lot. It's important to remember.

Social media, when used properly, is an excellent way to engage with your members. It allows you to have conversations, which leads to relationships and trusted communities.

I like to say that social media engagement is a lot like dating. You wouldn't marry someone the moment you meet them (unless, of course, you're a contestant on that dreadful reality TV show!). You start off at home, doing nothing. Then you might observe who is out there. Is it worth getting off the couch and away from the TV and Tim Tams to go on a date? Once you decide that yes, maybe it is, you might get dressed up to go to the pub. Or you might create a profile on an online dating site. Or you might tell your friends you're ready to start dating again and ask if they have any suitable single friends.

Sooner or later, you'll go on a date, where, presumably, you'll have that getting-to-know-you conversation. Yes, some of these will be a lot more awkward than others (no, I'm not sharing my first-date experiences here – but let me tell you, I've had my share of awkward ones!). Once you've found someone you want to continue the conversation with, you'll have a second date, then a third, and before you know it, you really like each other and you're in a relationship (!). And, in time, you might create your own little community by moving in together, or getting married, and maybe even having kids.

USING SOCIAL MEDIA TO ENGAGE MEMBERS		
Social Media Use	**Benefit**	**Engagement**
Community	Trusted	10x
Relationships	Liked	8x
Conversation	Known	5x
Broadcasting	Promoting	2x
Observing	Learning	0x
Doing nothing	No value	-10x

Two-way — Community, Relationships, Conversation
One-way — Broadcasting, Observing

© Mel Kettle

Let's have a look at the Social Media Engagement Ladder and determine where your association sits.

DOING NOTHING

At the bottom of the ladder, you're doing nothing. You're offering no value to your members via social media. This means you are

missing valuable opportunities to engage with your members. It's possible you're not using social media because you don't know where to start, or you simply don't believe it has value.

However, while you're doing nothing, your members are wondering where you are. Remember that 79% of Australians[16] use social media regularly, and they have an expectation that you also use it.

Reading this book is a fantastic way to get started. It will guide you through the process of identifying which social channels your members use and how to create a plan. It will also provide you with the tools you need to incorporate social media into your communication schedule in a way that won't take up all your time.

OBSERVING

As you begin to use social media, observe how other associations use it. What channels do they use? Do they engage with their members? How do they demonstrate the value of membership? What types of content do they create and share? How do their members and broader audience respond to them? While it's important to observe and learn, try not to spend too much time in this phase. Start thinking about how you can use social media within your association to engage and demonstrate value to your members.

If you're not sure who to follow online, start with your members and colleagues, your peers, other associations in your industry, relevant media organisations and politicians. For more ideas, search hashtags on Twitter and Instagram – try #associations and #assnchat to start with.

---

16 Sensis Pty Ltd. *Sensis Social Media Report 2017*, Melbourne, 2017.
https://www.sensis.com.au/socialmediareport (accessed 25 October, 2017).

BROADCASTING

The broadcasting level is also known as "let's-spam-them-with-as-much-sales-information-about-our-association-as-we-can-and-hope-they-immediately-sign-up-for-membership".

While it's great you're starting to have an online presence, at this level there is no conversation. Engagement is negligible and you're not generating feelings of goodwill. All you're doing is distributing your marketing material, which is a one-way communication. In other words, it's advertising – and advertising gets boring quickly. It's rarely successful as an engagement tactic. Usually, all advertising does is annoy your audience, and, frankly, the people who took the time to follow you deserve a whole lot better. Yes, it's a touchpoint, but for most people, it's akin to spam emails.

So, what should you do instead? Try to move quickly through this phase to the next level, so you can start having conversations with your followers and initiate conversations with people who interest you.

CONVERSATION

This level is where we start to move from one-way conversations to two-way conversations. Real engagement with your audience begins to take place as they get to know you. It's loads of fun, as you get to find out a whole lot about your members and they get to learn more about the real you. And by "you", I mean you as the individual/s running the account, as well as you the association.

The key word in the phrase "social media" is *social* – so it's critical we have conversations. They are an essential part of becoming known. Please don't feel all conversations need to have a heavy business focus. The strongest business relationships I have built on social media started with social conversations about food, TV shows (*MasterChef* and *The Voice* – please don't judge me!), local and global events, more food, the weather and little things that annoy me (teenagers who put the peanut butter back in the cupboard when the jar is essentially empty, and who don't write it on the shopping list! ARGH! And now you know what I tried to have for breakfast today … BTW it's ALWAYS crunchy.).

If you share content as @yournameCEO, then sharing some of these more personal topics will humanise you. If you share content as @associationname, then you need to identify other ways to personalise your content. This could include sharing stories about what goes on behind the scenes, staff celebrations, a day in the life of your CEO, what everyone's choice of coffee or tea is, etc. The idea is to take the focus away from business and put it on more personal topics your audience can relate to. This helps you build a rapport with them.

RELATIONSHIPS

Once you move on from casual conversations, relationships start to form. This is when people start to like you. Relationships become more committed as your audience likes you and your brand more. Engagement increases and it's during this stage that positive word of mouth usually starts to occur.

COMMUNITY

The shift from relationships to the community level happens when organisations realise the benefits of providing value for others versus taking the value for themselves. At this level, when value is given without expectation, trust is maximised. It's important to remember communities and trust aren't built overnight – they take time and energy.

Remember how the bookstore Avid Reader effectively dealt with trolls? There is no way it could have done this had it not spent time and energy building its community. Have a look at Avid Reader's social media accounts, in particular, Facebook (www.facebook.com/avidreaderbookshop) and Twitter (@avidreader4101), and you will see how it takes the time to share its followers' content and engage in conversation.

WHAT MAKES SUCCESSFUL SOCIAL MEDIA?

With the average person having an attention span shorter than that of a goldfish, it's critical we get our social media content right. There are three key elements to successful social media communication (these apply to all forms of communication, but because this book is about social media, that's what I'll talk about):

1. Customer
2. Content
3. Channel

You must deliver the right content to the right customer via the right channel. This may not seem difficult, but for many organisations, it is.

It's a bit like fly fishing. Years ago, my English uncle, a keen fly fisherman, explained the sport to me as we prepared for a salmon-fishing expedition to Scotland (an hour or two from his home). I was 22 and super excited about trying something he was so passionate about. Plus, I was excited about the prospect of salmon for dinner (it's a fave!).

My uncle spent a long time explaining how to tie a fly, and what all the other bits and pieces did. He explained how to cast, how to spot where the fish might be, and where the fly should land. He told me if I wanted to have the best possible chance of catching a fish, I had to use the right rod to cast the right fly in the right spot at the right time. If I didn't do these things the right way, I would end up scaring the fish away.[17]

Social media has similar parallels. If you don't create content of value to your members using the channels they prefer, they won't be able to connect with you.

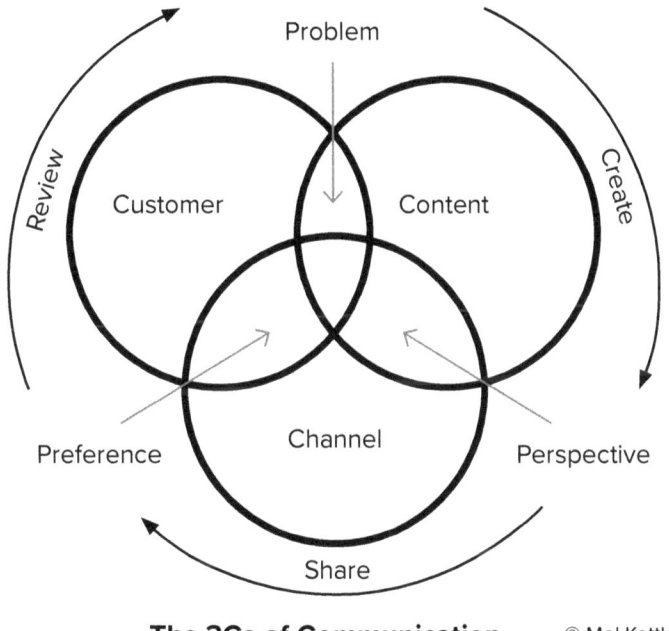

The 3Cs of Communication   © Mel Kettle

---

17 I know you desperately want to know how many salmon we caught that day. Sadly, the weather was miserable, so we decided to go to Whitby for a fish-and-chips lunch in a cosy pub instead. And Uncle Michael bought me my first Guinness. I'll never forget that day. And I still haven't been to Scotland. And I really want to. So, if you're a Scottish association and want me to come and do some work with you, please let me know! You can email me at mel@melkettle.com :)

Let's look at these three elements more closely.

1. CUSTOMER

"Get closer than ever to your customers. So close that you tell them what they need well before they realise it themselves."
– Steve Jobs

Managing the customer (your member) is the most important of the 3Cs of successful social media communication. You need to know their problems so you can provide a solution. Listen to what your members are saying online. Find out how you can help them.

It's important you show them how much you respect and value them by giving them what they want (content that is of value to them). Most importantly, you need to engage with them on the channels they use. It's critical you:

- Know your brand values and what your association stands for.

- Are focused on your brand. Make sure your brand values are clear in all your online and offline communication.

- Respond to comments and queries. There is no point saying how much you respect your members if you don't reply to them when they comment on your social channels.

- Are authentic. Keep it real and don't be afraid to show off your personality (and your association's!). This helps build trust.

2. CONTENT

The content you share is your social media currency. It needs to be shareable, valuable and relatable. Good content also solves your members' problems. Share content – either created or curated – that cuts through the clutter. I will go into a lot more detail about content in Chapter 4.

Your members will have different learning perspectives. Are they visual, auditory, kinaesthetic or tactile? Your content creation and channel selection must reflect each of these senses. Don't only rely on text – use images, video and audio to help get your message across.

Put processes in place to regularly review your content. Measure what works and what doesn't. One of the best things about social media is that because it's online, you can measure and analyse everything. There is a lot more information about what and how to measure in Chapter 6.

3. CHANNEL

Finally, which channels do your members use? Go there. Choose your online and offline channels based on where your audience is, how they prefer to receive information and the nature of the information you need to communicate.

According to research by Social Media Examiner,[18] marketers identify Facebook as the single most important social media channel for business-to-business (B2B) and business-to-consumer (B2C) businesses. In fact, in 2017, Facebook surpassed LinkedIn as the most important platform for B2B marketers.

---

18 Social Media Examiner. *2017 Social Media Marketing Industry Report*, May 2017. https://www.socialmediaexaminer.com/social-media-marketing-industry-report-2017/

All your members have preferences as to how they are communicated with. Adhering to these preferences when determining which channels to use means they are more likely to hear and act on your message.

SOCIAL MEDIA USE IN AUSTRALIA

We have been fortunate in Australia over the past few years: Sensis has undertaken an annual survey of Australian consumers, small-to-medium businesses and large businesses to find out how they use social networking sites, including Facebook, LinkedIn, Twitter and Instagram. The report usually comes out in June each year. It is well worth keeping an eye out for as its data is invaluable. #notsponsored

The *Sensis Social Media Report 2017* reveals current data, compares data back to 2011 and looks at changing trends. It will help you identify where your members are, how they use social media, when and where they use it, and what they expect from the brands they follow.

Below is a summary of the more useful, and sometimes quirky, data from the 2017 report. I highly recommend you download and read the report in full – it's an easy read, with many of the results explained in plain language. You do not need to be a data nerd to understand it and extrapolate its use to your organisation! You can download the report from www.sensis.com.au/about/our-reports/sensis-social-media-report.

KEY STATS:

- 99% of Australians have an internet-enabled device (we average three each).

- 81% own a smartphone (59% laptop, 51% desktop, 45% tablet). In terms of age, 99% of 18-29-year olds and 96% of 30-39-year olds own a smartphone. Think about the implications for your organisation if you target these age groups, yet your website is not enabled for mobile.

- 84% of Aussies access the internet daily, with 56% accessing the internet more than five times a day.

- 79% use social networking sites (up from 69% in 2016), and 35% check social media more than five times a day.

WHERE WE USE SOCIAL MEDIA:

- 57% use social media first thing in the morning, 18% when commuting, 21% during work (this seems quite low to me), 47% on breaks, 47% at lunchtime, 71% after work/in the evening, and 39% last thing before bed. This changes quite a lot depending on the age group. For example, 79% of 18-29-year olds check social media first thing in the morning, compared to 43% of 50-64-year olds.

- 96% use social media at home compared with 35% at work, 43% on public transport, 33% at restaurants/bars/parties, 37% in the car (I hope this isn't while driving, although I suspect for far too many it is), 16% at sporting events and 14% while on the loo (!!!). Interestingly, 17% of males use it on the toilet compared to 12% of females, and 29% of these are 18-29-year olds. Yes, I also said ewwww!

- About 35% use social media while watching TV, with 43% of these people watching reality TV.

THE SITES WE USE:

- Social networking sites used were Facebook (94%), YouTube (51%), Instagram (46%), Snapchat (40%), Twitter (32%), LinkedIn (18%) and Pinterest (10%).

- In terms of messaging services, 81% use Facebook Messenger, 34% use Viber, 18% use WhatsApp and 12% don't use any form of messaging service.

- The typical user spends almost 10 hours a week on Facebook.

- Males are more connected than females, with males having 522 friends, contacts or followers compared to 418 for females. This is across Facebook, LinkedIn, Twitter, Instagram, Snapchat and Google+. The younger the age group, the more friends, contacts or followers.

- Smartphones are by far the most preferred device for social networking, with 81% of users accessing social media via a smartphone (a steady increase since 2011). This compares to 30% accessing it on a laptop, 28% on a desktop and 25% on a tablet.

- Why do people use social media? Not surprisingly, 89% said to catch up with friends and family, 43% said to watch videos, 26% said to find or connect with people with the same interests, 18% said to find out about brands/ businesses, 16% said to research products or services, and 9% said to engage with brands for customer-service reasons.

- Advertising isn't the taboo you might expect, with 30% of people quite happy to see ads on social networking sites (however, 30% are not). 57% ignore sponsored posts from businesses they don't follow.

- 37% will inspect a brand's social media presence before making a purchase.

WHAT ARE AUSTRALIAN BUSINESSES DOING ON SOCIAL MEDIA?

Now, here is the good stuff. What are Australian businesses doing on social media? Let me tell you right now, not enough of you are using it. And you should be.

- 53% of small businesses are not on social media, compared to 51% of medium businesses and 40% of large businesses.

- The businesses that do use social media primarily use Facebook, Twitter and LinkedIn.

- Large businesses (95%) mostly use social media for two-way communication with clients and contacts – this is up from 76% in 2016, and a model that small and medium-sized businesses need to follow.

- Only 36% of small businesses that use social media update every day (up from 23% in 2016).

- Most businesses do not measure their social media return on investment. If this is you, make sure you read Chapter 6 on measurement and analytics.

- Only 40% of small businesses and 43% of medium-sized businesses have a social media strategy. If you're not in this category, you need to read Chapter 2 – Strategic Thinking.

WHAT DOES THIS MEAN FOR YOUR ASSOCIATION?

Plenty of things.

- If you are not using social media, you need to be. Your members are there, and you are missing out on some excellent opportunities to engage with them. Social media is awesome for providing excellence in customer service – read Chapter 3 on Customer Service to find out more.

- If you only promote your business during work hours, say, 9am-5pm or even 8am-6pm, you miss valuable opportunities to engage, given most people use social media when they wake up and after work. This means you need to do some serious rethinking. You don't need to be on social media 24/7, but you need to have more than just a 9-5 presence.

- Given the clear majority of people use Facebook (95%), it's vital that you consider Facebook as a marketing tool. The significantly smaller usage of other social media channels is a clear indication that you need to know who your target market is and where they are likely to be.

- Write a social media strategy. If you use social media but don't have a strategy, you're wasting your time and energy. Your plan needs to link to your overarching business strategy and marketing plan. Read Chapter 2 for more information on how to do this.

- Be aware of social media demographics, and how and where they access it. Know the demographics of your target market and know where they are. Be responsive to them. Increasingly, there is the expectation that businesses are on social media, so you need a valid reason if you are not. "I'm too scared" or "I can't be bothered" doesn't cut it.

Another great source of data is the Pew Research Center based in the USA. It is a non-partisan fact tank that informs the public about issues, attitudes and trends shaping the world. Its researchers conduct public opinion polling, demographic research, content analysis and other data-driven social science research. It has a lot of useful information on many topics – you can find its social media information here: www.pewinternet. org/fact-sheet/social-media.

OVERVIEW OF THE FIVE KEY SKILLS

This book has been written to help you better understand why social media is important for associations, and to provide you with guidance to either get started or improve how you incorporate social media into your marketing and membership activities.

In this book, I share the five key skills you need to increase member engagement, generate a return on investment and create a thriving online community. I also explain why these skills are important and how you can develop them.

The five key skills are:

1. Strategic thinking
2. Customer service focused
3. Having a creative mindset
4. Being organised
5. An ability to analyse

Each skill has a chapter dedicated to it. You will quickly realise that each skill is relevant to many aspects of association management, not just social media. You can use these skills in all your marketing communications, as well as to improve your membership, human resources, finance and broader business strategies.

This book will not teach you how to use Facebook, Twitter, LinkedIn or any other social channel. However, I do offer advice on creating content, using influencers, generating social proof, establishing a consistent voice, managing the demands of being a community manager, how to save time and be more productive, and how to determine success and value. To learn the day-to-day practicalities of each channel, the best resources include blogs, videos and podcasts. The ins and outs of most social media channels change frequently, meaning books become outdated before they are even printed! I've listed some useful resources at the back of this book in the Resources section.

To demonstrate the rapidly changing nature of social media, in the past week alone (today is 13 November, 2017), the following changes have been announced:

- Twitter has rolled out a 280-character limit to all accounts.

- Twitter has announced new rules to improve user safety and experience and clarified how it will deal with hate speech and harassment in the future.

- Polls have been introduced for Facebook pages.

- Instagram is testing a tool to add older images to Stories.

- Facebook Messenger has a new chat plugin.

QUESTIONS FOR YOU TO CONSIDER

1. Where do you see your association in five years' time?

_____

_____

_____

2. Who will your members be?

_____

_____

_____

3. Where are you on the Social Media Engagement Ladder?

_____

_____

_____

4. What do you need to do to move higher up the ladder?

_____

_____

_____

_____

5. What communication channels are you currently using?

_____

_____

_____

6. What social media channels are you currently using?

_____

_____

_____

7. Do your current communication activities meet the needs of all your members?

_____

_____

_____

8. What do you fail to deliver on by not using social media?

_____

_____

_____

9. How are other associations using social media?

_____

_____

_____

10. What channels do they use?

_____

_____

_____

11. Do they engage with their members?

_____

_____

_____

_____

12. How do they demonstrate the value of membership?

_____

_____

_____

_____

13. What types of content do they create and share?

_____

_____

_____

_____

14. How do their members and broader audience respond to them?

_____

_____

_____

_____

CHAPTER 2

KEY SKILL 1: STRATEGIC THINKING

"Strategic thinking rarely occurs spontaneously."
– Michael Porter

_____

WHAT IS STRATEGIC THINKING?

In the early stages of my career, I often heard the phrase, "You need to think more strategically." I didn't really understand what it meant.

So, what do I mean when I say strategic thinking is one of the five key skills you need to become a social association?

To me, strategic thinking is an ongoing process that connects what has happened in the past with the information you have today and links this with your expectations for tomorrow. It happens when you think about opportunities and challenge assumptions. Non-strategic thinkers are likely to say, "We have always done things this way," or, "Let's not rock the boat," whereas a strategic thinker will say, "Why don't we try [insert new way of doing things]?" or, "Could we do things differently?"

It's not easy to be a strategic thinker, especially in such a rapidly changing world. New technologies appear every week, and, as communication professionals, we need to at least be aware of what is happening so we can assess what's right for our associations.

Strategic thinking isn't a skill only held by senior managers and leaders. Everyone in your organisation can, and should, learn to think strategically.

The three key actions that will help you become a more strategic thinker are:

1. Be aware of current trends.
2. Take time out to think and reflect.
3. Ask questions.

These key actions are outlined below in more detail.

1. BE AWARE OF CURRENT TRENDS

You need to be aware of trends within your industry, the association and/or not-for-profit sector, and the broader environment. Consider the benefits and consequences for your organisation.

In terms of the broader environment, look at what's happening in the economic, social, environmental, legal, political, technological and demographic spheres. What happens if there is a change of government (in Australia as well as in other countries)? What is the impact of legislative change? What is the effect of economic change, such as inflation, employment and currency fluctuations?

Key trends to be alert to include: the increase in urbanisation, the advent of "smart" products, greater global connectivity, an aging population, and the rising cost of energy and water. How do these impact your organisation, sector and members?

In 2018, it's vital we are attentive to technological trends – in particular, the growing use of augmented reality, the ever-increasing popularity of video (specifically, Instagram Stories and live streaming), and the buying power of Gen Z (those born after 1996) and their use of Instagram and Snapchat. Looking at Gen Z for a moment, the *Sensis Social Media Report 2017*[1] indicates 81% of Australians aged 18-29 use Instagram and 77% use Snapchat. So, if you're targeting this age group but not using these channels, you need to rethink your strategy.

2. TAKE TIME OUT TO THINK AND REFLECT

Only twice in my years as an employee did I have a manager who regularly carved out time from their work schedule to think strategically and reflect. One manager allocated two consecutive days a month, another allocated three hours a week. These times were diarised at the start of each year and they were sacrosanct. The benefits of this time were immeasurable: it gave clarity to our work, allowed us to see what our competitors and colleagues were doing, and helped us examine the broader environment we worked in.

During this time, the managers engaged in a number of key activities: they read widely from industry and business texts (magazines, journals, blogs and books); they spoke to people doing interesting things in their industry and sector; they assimilated their thinking into new ideas or tightened old ideas; and they held regular strategic planning sessions with their team to stimulate ideas from those of us at the "coal face" of the organisation.

---

1 Sensis Pty Ltd. *Sensis Social Media Report 2017*, Melbourne 2017. https://www.sensis. com.au/socialmediareport (accessed 25 October, 2017).

I know that when I take time out to look around and think ahead, my practice benefits. The best place for me to think strategically and reflect is when I'm away from my office. I try to allocate time to read every day, often in the morning over breakfast or while having lunch. Some days, I only have time to read a couple of blog posts via Twitter, or a LinkedIn article or two. Other days, I have an hour to read the better part of a book. I'm currently trialling the app Blinkist (www.blinkist.com), which provides short insights into best-selling non-fiction books. These insights can be read in about 15 minutes or listened to via the audio option. If I like what I read in the synopsis, I can choose to buy the book and read it in full.

Dan Norris, in his excellent book, *Create or Hate*, says: "Most of our creative effort happens when we're not working. Relaxation is the key to unleashing the power of creativity."

Our ideas tend to flow when we are relaxed. Indeed, research from Stanford University found that going for a walk can improve creativity by as much as 60%.[2]

Personally, I have my best ideas when I'm travelling, relaxing at our family holiday house, in the shower, lying in bed trying to sleep at 3am (yep, peri-menopause is good for that!) and on my daily walk (sans device).

3. ASK QUESTIONS

Not only do I want you to ask questions, but I want you to ask the hard questions. You know the ones. Do we all know what we are working to achieve? What does value really look like to our members? What works with our member offering? How can

---

2 Jabr, F. "Why walking helps us think", *The New Yorker*, 3 September, 2017. https://www.newyorker.com/tech/elements/walking-helps-us-think (accessed 31 October, 2017).

we be better? Do we have the right people doing the right jobs? What will our association look like in five years? In 10 years? Will we still be around if we continue to do what we have always done?

Think about how you can be a better and more effective strategic thinker. What can you do differently? Can you shape your day/week/month to allow time to think and reflect? What are some of the questions you need to ask within your organisation?

WHAT IS STRATEGIC PLANNING?

Strategic planning and strategic thinking go hand in hand. They are not the same, but they are close cousins.

Strategic planning is a process that relies on strategic thinking. Where strategic thinking considers what the solution to a problem is, strategic planning creates a structured process (such as a communication and social media strategy) to solve the problem.

Taking the time to develop your strategic planning processes will allow you to develop a more clearly thought-out social media strategy. This will go a long way towards transforming your organisation into a social association. It will help you determine your social media goals and objectives, understand your target market, and make decisions about what content to create and when and how to share it.

It's important to remember that social media is a marketing and customer-service tool – just as a website, brochure and an exhibition booth are tools. You must be strategic with how you use it. Being strategic with your communication and social media means you will find it far easier to make decisions about what and when to post, as you will have greater clarity on who your audience is and where and when they hang out. Social media expert and not-for-profit specialist Andrea Rowe (www.yourcoastalconnection.com.au) agrees, saying: "A social media strategy provides the team with a rational and reasonable process to follow, and helps you focus on your core values and core mission."

It is easy to be swayed by new technologies, tactics and content. However, if you have a clear strategy, you can stay focused on what is relevant so you can achieve your overarching goals.

GET SUPPORT FROM THE CEO AND BOARD

Quite often, people come to me and say, "We really need to use social media in our organisation, but I'm struggling to get buy-in and support from my senior management team (or the board)." Does that sound familiar?

If you want to create a business case for using social media, there are a few things you need to know:

- **The numbers.** *The Sensis Social Media Report* can help you with this. In Chapter 1, I gave an overview of the key statistics, but you will need to delve a little further into the report to work out what numbers you need to help make your case.

- **Market and audience trends.** What's happening in your industry and the broader environment in terms of social media? Can you capitalise on these trends?

- **Your audience.** Talk to your members and broader audience, either one on one or by running a couple of focus groups (use a web-based meeting tool, such as Zoom

Meetings, to reach people in a broad geographical region). Find out where they are and what they expect from you in terms of social media use. Gain an understanding of which audience segments would be supportive of your proposal, and use this data to show value.

- **Your association's mission statement and values.** What do you fail to deliver on by not using social media?

- **Your clearly articulated reason for wanting a social media presence.** It could be to provide better service to your members so they experience the same level of service online as they do face to face, or it could be another reason.

Association executive Robert Barnes[3] suggests building a business case using the terms your CEO/board normally uses to make decisions, but base it on the data you want to present. Place a value on the proposed change – money saved, time saved, productivity increased, etc. Barnes says you need to dehumanise the business case so a decision is based on its purpose, not the people involved.

Barnes also suggests asking for the money and/or time to conduct an experiment rather than the whole enchilada. For example, start using one social media channel. Do a cost-benefit analysis and forecast what you expect the results will be based on your research. Measure everything so you can demonstrate how your experiment succeeded.

When I first started working, I worked for a small conference management company. Whenever I wanted to try something new or spend money on something, all I had to do was ask my boss and give her 2-3 reasons why. She would then say yes or no. It rarely took more than a few minutes (some of the bigger asks

---

3 www.linkedin.com/in/robertmbarnes

might have been thought about for a day or two), and as I usually had a valid reason, the answer was quite often yes.

My second job was with a large multinational, and every decision needed to be requested in writing. Decisions often took weeks, due to a policy stipulating that major decisions had to be made by our head office in the USA. It was a painful experience for someone who was accustomed to verbally asking a question and getting an immediate answer.

When I worked in government, I had to write briefing notes to explain what we wanted to do and ask for money for the project. Granted, the money I wanted was a whole lot more than what I asked for in job #1, but the process was exponentially more tedious. What it did teach me, however, was to learn to ask for what I wanted in a way that would give me the best possible likelihood of getting a yes. This included knowing the numbers and knowing the pros and cons of going forward with the project, as well as the pros and cons of not going forward with it. For example, what was the risk to our reputation if we didn't implement a particular project?

Entrepreneur Richard Branson suggests finding as many downsides to an idea as possible. Look at these downsides and risks, and propose a mitigation strategy for each. Do your homework so you have an answer to every negative question thrown at your proposal. The more prepared you are, the more likely you are to get a yes – especially if you place a value on the proposed change and ensure the business case has a specific purpose.

HOW TO WRITE A SOCIAL MEDIA STRATEGY

"If your foundation isn't right, you have no chance
of long-term success."
– Gary Vaynerchuk

A well thought-out social media strategy is an essential tool for the social association. However, it should not be written in isolation – first and foremost, it needs to strategically align with your overarching business strategy, your marketing communication strategy and your membership strategy. You also need to consider your mission and values, so these transfer to your social media activity.

By the end of this section, you will have a thorough understanding of how to write a social media strategy. Be aware that it doesn't need to be 20, 30 or 40 pages long. Some of the more successful strategies I've seen, particularly for smaller associations, are only three to four pages.

However, all social media strategies should include the following key sections:

- **Introduction and any relevant research.** If your social media strategy needs to be signed off by your senior management team or board, and they don't have a strong understanding of the value of using social media, then consider including data from the *Sensis Social Media Report* outlining how Australians use social media. This is also where you should include an overview of environmental and market trends, an analysis of other associations in your sector, and an overview of where your organisation sits with its current social media use.

Other information for this section includes: how your social media strategy aligns with your strategic, marketing and membership plans; a brief overview of the social media activities you currently undertake; and any internal issues you need to highlight (such as current staffing levels, attitude towards social media, etc.).

- **Goals.** What do you want to your social media strategy to achieve? You want your goals to be SMART – specific, measurable, agreed upon, realistic and time based. Remember, these goals are specifically for social media. For example: boosting brand awareness by increasing the number of Facebook likes on your page by 30% over 12 months; expanding your social media reach by 20% over 12 months; improving brand engagement by 30% over 12 months (measured by the number of likes, comments and shares on your social media posts).

- **Target audience.** It's important you are clear on who your target audience is, as this impacts the type of content you create and where you share it. Segment your target audience into:

  – **Demographics:** Age, gender, where they live/work, how educated they are, where they are in their career.
  – **Geography:** Are they local (i.e. a suburb, city or a specific regional area), national or international.
  – **Psychographics:** Look at what they value. What are their attitudes towards your industry, sector and organisation? Also consider whether they are current members, past members or never members.

  Know when and where your audience hangs out on social media. Be as specific as you can, as this will save you time and money when developing content to solve their problems.

- **Digital landscape.** Your digital landscape (see diagram) represents where you have a presence online. At the centre of this is your website, with all the other elements either driving traffic to your website or taking content from your website. Identify where social media fits in, and which channels you might use.

  If you don't currently have a website, that should be your first priority, as it needs to be the home for your content. You don't own your social media space – meaning, you don't own your space on Facebook, Twitter, Instagram or LinkedIn. Putting all your content solely on your social media channels is like building a house on land you don't own. You just wouldn't!

  The diagram on the following page shows what a digital landscape might look like for a member-based organisation.

- **Social media channels and tactics.** There are many social media channels you can use, and I talk more about the common channels further in this chapter. If you are new to social media, I strongly suggest you start with just one. If you have clearly identified your target audience, you should have a good understanding of where they hang out. Most associations will either choose Facebook or LinkedIn as their social media starting point. For each channel you choose, identify the audience, how frequently you will post, the purpose of posting to that channel, the type of content, any budget required, and how you will measure success.

- **Risk analysis.** A lot of the associations I have worked with are highly risk averse, so a risk analysis can help mitigate fear. Demonstrate you have thought about what could go wrong, and articulate the steps you will take to mitigate the risks. See Table 2.1 for a sample risk analysis.

Digital landscape

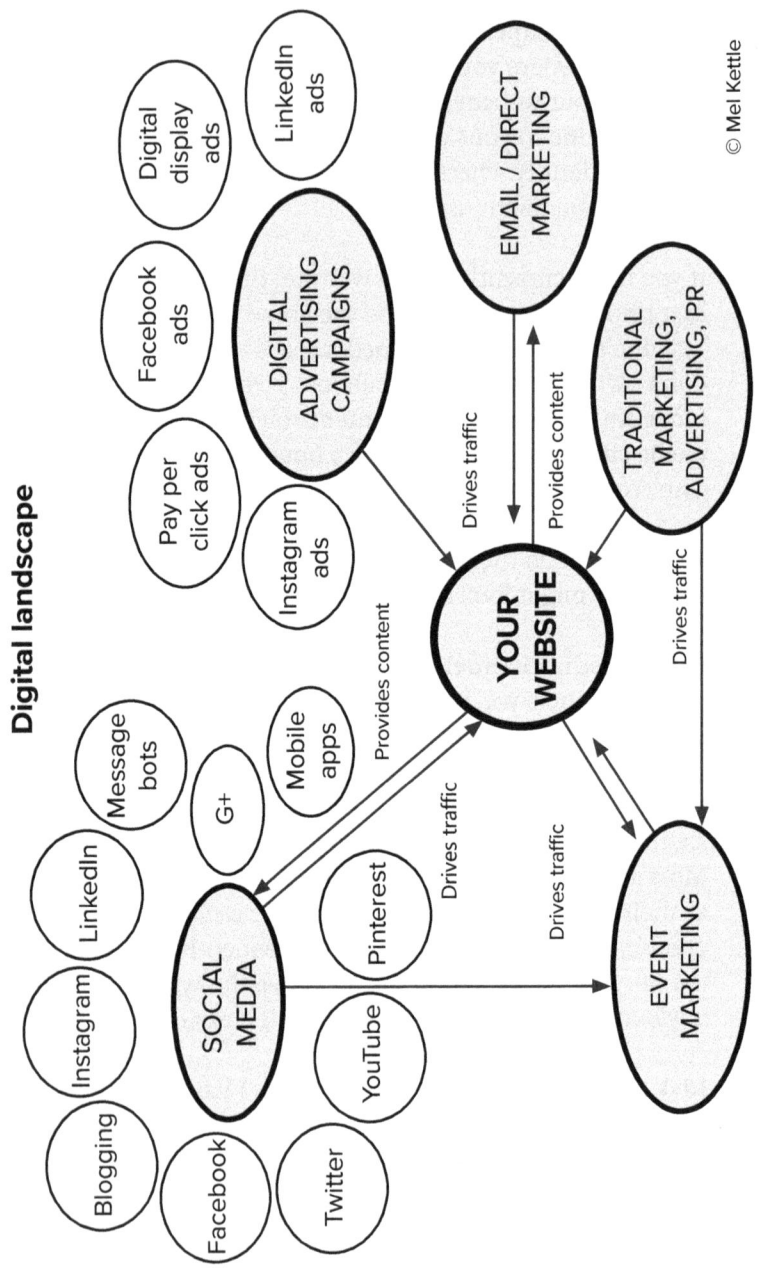

© Mel Kettle

- **Resource management.** Although it's free to use social media platforms such as Facebook, Twitter, LinkedIn and the rest, there is a cost in terms of time. Many organisations outsource elements of their social media management, which costs money. And then there are fees for third-party tools that make life easier – tools such as image-creation and editing sites; video-editing software; stock photos or photo shoots; scheduling tools; and social listening tools. How much or how little you use these tools depends on the size of your organisation, and whether you can get by with free versions or require more sophisticated and expensive paid versions. But associations generally don't need a big budget for social media – there's a lot you can do with a little money and a lot of ingenuity.

- **An action plan.** Arguably, the action plan is the most important part of your strategy. In its most simple form, your action plan is a to-do list. More sophisticated action plans include fancy Excel spreadsheets with many columns. Regardless of what you choose, your action plan should set out who does what and when, what and how content is created, where and when it is posted, and the metrics for each. Make sure everyone responsible for an action knows what is expected of them. Encourage your team to schedule activities into a calendar, pin them on the wall next to their desk, or use an app that reminds them. It doesn't matter how great your strategy is if no action is taken!

- **Measurement and metrics.** Your social media strategy should include metrics that gauge likes, comments and shares, reach, the nature of engagement (positive, negative, supportive, etc.), and the traffic driven to your website. You also want to measure the impact in terms of sales, such as new members, renewing members and event registration. Analytics and numbers are discussed in more detail in Chapter 6.

Table 2.1: Sample risk analysis

RISK	RISK MITIGATION	RISK OWNER
• No social media presence resulting in a lack of credibility. • Poor member service. • Inability to respond to feedback.	• Create a social media strategy and get started!	• Communication department.
• Failure to use social media appropriately.	• Create a social media policy. • Train staff on how to use social media. • Work with senior managers and the board on the importance of brand. • Maintain open and transparent communication. • Develop a social media training module for new staff. • Create an internal communication strategy.	• Communication department.

Continued next page

From previous page

RISK	RISK MITIGATION	RISK OWNER
• Confidential information posted on social media.	• Stipulate terms in the employment contract. • Update confidentiality policy. • Create a social media policy. • Develop a social media training module for new staff. • Incorporate in code of conduct.	• Communication department. • HR.
• Operational risks – the risk of loss resulting from inadequate or failed internal processes, people and systems, or from external events, such as phishing or malware.	• Train staff around digital scams and cyber criminals. • Include in staff induction.	• IT department.

Continued next page

From previous page

RISK	RISK MITIGATION	RISK OWNER
• Reputation risks due to careless posting to social media and/or deliberate sabotage.	• Training for ALL staff about what is acceptable to post on social media about the organisation (on official and personal accounts, link back to Code of Conduct). • Code of conduct awareness. • Employment contract. • Confidentiality policy. • Social media policy. • Develop a social media training module for new staff.	• Communication department. • HR.

Continued next page

From previous page

RISK	RISK MITIGATION	RISK OWNER
• Loss of management control of digital information that may result in it being degraded, lost or inappropriately accessed.	• Document the business purpose of major digital information assets. • Document and assign roles and responsibilities for management of the digital information. • Ensure mechanisms are in place for addressing changes in technology and/or responsibilities. • Plan for the end of contracts with vendors, staff and contractors. Ensure the contracts address the current and future control of the digital information, for example, post-contract.	• IT department. • Marketing and communication.

CASE STUDY

The Creche & Kindergarten Association Limited (C&K) has almost 400 services throughout Queensland providing early childhood education and care, including child care and kindergarten. Feedback from services and parents helped C&K realise that while it had an effective marketing strategy, it had little emphasis on digital communication and social media. Consequently, it was missing out on branding and marketing opportunities to its target market, which has a strong online presence (especially on Facebook).

I worked closely with the C&K marketing and communications team to develop a social media strategy that aligned with its strategic plan and marketing and communications plan.

THE STRATEGY IDENTIFIED:

- Core reasons why C&K needed a greater digital presence, which were presented to the board and management team.

- Which social channels to focus on in the immediate term, short term and long term.

- Tactics that would raise C&K's digital profile to provide "quick wins", as well as longer-term strategies.

THE OUTCOMES:

- C&K now has a significantly stronger communication presence within the digital space, and it is the market

Continued next page

From previous page

leader for Queensland child-care services with regards to digital communication. This has resulted in increased brand awareness and enrolments.

- In approximately 12 months, C&K significantly increased its social media presence, following and engagement, particularly on Facebook and Twitter. It now also uses Instagram, LinkedIn and Pinterest, with a mix of content including written, visual and video.

- There is a clear policy around who is responsible within C&K for managing the corporate social media accounts, and the 400-plus services are aware of their roles and responsibilities in terms of social media.

- A dedicated team member is solely focused on managing social media and the digital strategy.

HOW TO IDENTIFY THE RIGHT SOCIAL MEDIA CHANNELS FOR YOUR ASSOCIATION

One of the most common questions I am asked is, "Which social media channels should I use?" If you aren't social media savvy (yet!), it can be overwhelming. Which channel do I choose? Where do I start? How many do I use at once? The simple answer is: use the ones where your target audience hangs out. The tricky part can be working this out!

There are many options, but your main choices are Facebook, Instagram, Twitter, LinkedIn and Snapchat. You can also blog, podcast and create a YouTube channel to share videos.

As well as deciding on which social media channels to use, you need to decide how many accounts you want per channel. You will have your main association account (@associationname), but will your CEO, board chair or other key staff members also have a social media account linked to your association? If you have a socially savvy CEO, then encourage him/her to have a Twitter, LinkedIn and/or Instagram account that reflects their role and personality.

Personally, I think it's a great idea to have your CEO tweeting separately to your association account. Not only do your members increasingly expect them to be there, it provides an opportunity to truly engage in conversation and be responsive to them. It's no surprise that the CEOs of many Fortune 500 companies are active Twitter users, as it allows them to build trust and loyalty by being social.

Have a look at how these corporates and associations CEOs use Twitter:

- Richard Branson (Virgin) – @richardbranson

- Gary Vaynerchuk (Vayner Media) – @garyvee

- Cecile Richard (Planned Parenthood Federation of America) – @CecileRichards

- Alison Verhoeven (Australian Healthcare & Hospitals Association) – @AlisonVerhoeven

- Paul Marsh (AFL Players' Association) – @Marsh_Paul

When deciding which social channels to use, you need to consider:

- **Who is your audience?** Are they members, prospective members, staff, your board, your suppliers, media, educators, academics, politicians, or a combination or all of these?

- **Where does your desired audience hang out?** If you don't know, ask them. Conduct a survey, ask them in your newsletter, ask at your events, phone your key influencers and most active members and ask them.

As I have mentioned before, if you are just starting out, don't try to be everywhere at once. Choose one social media channel and get really good at it. Then look at another channel, get really good at that, then look at another one!

Regularly review what's working and what's not. After six to 12 months, make an executive decision: "Is this platform working for me still?" If it is, fantastic. Then you need to ask, "How can I keep it working for me and how can I make it better?"

If it's not working for you, have an honest look at why. Is it because you're not making any effort, don't have the time or your audience isn't there? Consider whether it's time to step back from that channel. If it's not helping you achieve your goals, there is absolutely no shame in leaving a platform you've put time and energy into. Quitting a social media channel is a sign of consolidation and strength. You're not still using a telex machine,[4] are you? So why would you continue using a social media channel that's not working for you? Think of it as you would any other business tactic. Some of them will work for a time and some of them won't.

But remember, if you stop using a social media channel, don't close the account. Instead, pop an explanation in your bio along the lines of, "We no longer tweet from this account, instead you can find us on Facebook and Instagram (insert the links)."

Regardless of which channels you choose, make sure you don't use them to replace your website. Use social media to drive traffic to your website, not replace it.

The following table gives you the pros and cons of each channel, and I provide more details regarding each in the pages that follow:

---

4 I was going to say fax machine, but I know some of you still use them ...

Table 2.2: Overview of the main social media channels

CHANNEL	PURPOSE	STRATEGY	TARGET AUDIENCE
Facebook	• Influence. • Some advocacy.	More social. Tends to focus on B2C. Many opportunities to communicate in an unobtrusive way. Organic reach is dropping, hard to get traction without an ad spend. Great space for sharing personality and people stories. Video is growing significantly. Use Facebook to educate, entertain and inspire with your own content and by sharing the content of others.	Most-used social media channel, covers all demographics. Women use it more than men (77% of users are female) and women aged over 50 is a fast-growing demographic. Rapidly growing in importance for B2B marketing.

Continued next page

From previous page

CHANNEL	PURPOSE	STRATEGY	TARGET AUDIENCE
LinkedIn	• Advocacy. • Establish thought leadership.	Business oriented. Tends to have a B2B focus. Excellent place to share business ideas. Keep it professional. Good for business networking.	Current/future employees, industry peers, university-educated professionals.
Twitter	• Influence. • Establish thought leadership. • Build relationships.	Good for connecting with journalists. Easy to share content and network. Quick response time is expected.	Media, members, slightly older demographic, more urban than rural.
Instagram	• Influence.	Uses hashtags. Excellent for visual brands. Fast growing. Video and stories rapidly growing. Owned by Facebook.	Influencers, slightly younger demographic.

Continued next page

From previous page

CHANNEL	PURPOSE	STRATEGY	TARGET AUDIENCE
Snapchat	• Influence.	Good to engage with people one on one.	A younger demographic.
Blogging	• Influence and advocacy. • Establish thought leadership.	Great opportunity to share your knowledge and position yourself as an expert. You own your blog if it's with your URL, whereas you don't own social channels.	All.
YouTube	• Influence. • Advocacy.	Video is rapidly increasing in popularity, & many people prefer it to reading. Excellent way to show personality and authenticity. Create a brand channel & custom brand experience.	All.

Continued next page

From previous page

CHANNEL	PURPOSE	STRATEGY	TARGET AUDIENCE
Podcasting	• Influence. • Advocacy. • Establish thought leadership.	Podcasting is rapidly gaining popularity. Its unique advantage is people can consume audio content while doing another activity (exercise, housework, driving, etc.). Like video, it's an excellent way to show personality and authenticity. Create a podcast for your association.	All.

WHY ASSOCIATIONS SHOULD USE:

FACEBOOK

Facebook is the most used social media channel. In fact, 94% of Australians who use social media have a Facebook account. It is increasingly being used for B2B communication, with 2017 research by Social Media Examiner[5] indicating that for the first time, marketers are turning to Facebook more than LinkedIn to undertake business to business (B2B) marketing.

Reasons to consider Facebook include:

- Facebook pages are a great way to showcase your association, however, be warned: organic reach – the number of people who see your posts through unpaid distribution – is dropping dramatically. Using video and Facebook live can help boost your organic reach.

- Facebook groups can be public, closed or secret, and are an excellent way to make an impact on your audience, especially if you don't have a budget for Facebook ads. Facebook groups provide the opportunity for far greater personal engagement than a Facebook page and tend to have greater reach. Be aware, however, that managing a group can be time consuming.

- Create a Facebook group for members only as a way of adding value to their membership.

- Promote your events by creating a Facebook event for each conference, workshop and activity you run.

---

5 Social Media Examiner. *2017 Social Media Marketing Industry Report*, May 2017. https://www.socialmediaexaminer.com/social-media-marketing-industry-report-2017/

- Ask questions and poll your members to find out their opinions on a range of topics.

- Create Facebook Live videos to provide truly unique content. Go behind the scenes at your conference or in your office to show what is happening in real time. Facebook Live is one of the best ways to be truly authentic with your communication. It's also extremely low cost if you shoot it from your smartphone (see Chapter 4 for tips on creating and editing video on your smartphone).

- Use Facebook as a promotional tool to publicise your conference, membership campaigns and other activities.

- Share your story using popular conventions such as #ThrowbackThursday or #FlashbackFriday.

- Facebook is a quick and easy way to provide member support and answer questions.

Professional Speakers Australia (PSA) recently ramped up its Facebook activity. It uses its Facebook page (www.facebook.com/professionalspeakersaustralia) to promote chapter and national events, share research, run competitions, ask questions, showcase member success, promote member-only benefits and more. PSA also has several Facebook groups, including one closed group for all members and closed groups for different chapters. Membership of these groups is restricted to PSA members only, and the engagement and camaraderie are seen by many members as a benefit of joining.

When I spoke recently to PSA National President for 2017 Warwick Merry CSP, he said: "PSA uses Facebook in a variety of ways, including to promote events, attract potential members and share our members' successes. One of its most powerful features is that it gives us the ability to communicate with members and have members communicate with each other without overwhelming their inboxes. This works for the greater community, as well as for smaller groups like sub-committees and the board. I suspect it will be part of our communication strategy well into PSA's future."

TWITTER

Twitter seems to be the "forgotten cousin" of social media. Recently, US digital expert and author Jay Baer shared the research finding that "the average engagement rate on Twitter for brands is now 0.049%."[6] This suggests Twitter's time has passed, but social media marketing expert Mark Schaefer suggests the opposite, saying Twitter "may be the most powerful real-time marketing research tool on the planet."[7] Yes, it's easy to question what to do.

The latest data tells us about three million Australians use Twitter regularly, which is less than Facebook, Instagram and Snapchat, but more than LinkedIn and Pinterest.

The main advantages Twitter has over the other social media channels are:

- People do business with people, and, just like face-to-face networking, Twitter helps you build rapport, which leads to conversations, relationships and engagement with your association. And when people engage with you, they see your value.

6 Baer, J. "Is Twitter in 2017 Even Worth the Trouble?" *Convince & Convert*, 6 September, 2017. http://www.convinceandconvert.com/social-media-strategy/is-twitter-in-2017-even-worth-the-trouble/ (accessed 13 November, 2017).

7 Schaefer, M. "What's the Twouble with Twitter Marketing?" *Mark Schaefer*, 18 September, 2017. https://www.businessesgrow.com/2017/09/18/twitter-marketing/ (accessed 13 November, 2017).

- Twitter is real-time – use it to alert your members and followers to new research, special offers and the latest information. Then share that information via your newsletter, other social channels and other forms of communication.

- Its keyword-search function is excellent, making it a great option for finding up-to-date information.

- You can follow your members on Twitter and listen to their conversations. What do they say about your industry, your association, their challenges and problems? Twitter is an excellent tool for learning about your members so you can help them solve their problems by providing relevant solutions.

- You can build relationships with the media. Most journalists and media outlets have a Twitter account and use it to find relevant stories and sources. Many politicians use it, too, to find out what is happening in their electorates and portfolios.

- Sharing your expertise on Twitter can help you and your association become known as experts in your field. This will lead to more media and other professional opportunities, which is particularly useful if your association plays an advocacy role.

- It allows you to deal with the critics. Jay Baer, in his book, *Hug Your Haters*, says 61% of frequent complainers use Twitter daily (compared with 33% who use Facebook daily). So, if people are going to complain about you, it's likely to be via Twitter. This means if you don't have a presence on Twitter, you can't manage or mitigate the problem.

- You can establish a hashtag for your association. This helps your members find each other (and you) so they can create their own community.

- You can use Twitter to promote your annual conference and other events – before, during and after. This will raise awareness of your event and the value of your association, and grow your social media influence. Create an event hashtag and encourage delegates to use it to promote the speakers, sponsors, your association and the knowledge shared.

- Encourage your CEO, board and other key people to have a Twitter account and use it to build relationships with key influencers in your sector.

INSTAGRAM

Instagram use is on the rise, with more than 7.7 million Australians signed up – an increase of 2.5 million people in 12 months. It's currently the second-most popular social media channel, behind Facebook. More than 60% of users log into Instagram every day, with the average Instagram user spending 25 minutes a day on the channel.

For those who aren't familiar with Instagram, it's a social networking app that allows you to share photos and video from your smartphone. You can take and edit photos in the app or share photos from your phone's camera roll. From a business perspective, it's an exceptionally useful app for sharing images and video of your products, business and people. It gives your audience a visual reference of who you are and what you do, which drives awareness, engagement and sales.

Instagram is an excellent social media channel to help build relationships and connect with your members and broader audience. It provides the opportunity for you to connect in a personal and real way. The connections you make on Instagram can feel more genuine than those you make on Facebook.

I've outlined a few reasons why you should consider adding Instagram to your social media mix:

- People do business with people, and just like face-to face-networking, Instagram helps you build rapport, which leads to conversations, relationships and engagement with your association. And when people engage with you, they see your value. Use Instagram to celebrate significant milestones (of your association, your people, your members and new member campaigns), and to share events and resources or services you sell.

- Instagram is a great way to connect visually with your audience. Use it to educate people about what you do within your community, showcase new products and demonstrate the services you provide. Share images and videos of your events, and create images and videos of the people involved in your association. This helps show your human side.

- Use it to educate your members. Consider how you can use Instagram as a tool to educate and provide useful industry and career-based information to your audience.

- The use of hashtags is common on Instagram, so make sure you use them in your posts. Hashtags make it far easier for your members to find you on Instagram than on Facebook. Some popular hashtags to consider include #association and #assnchat. Also, use industry-specific and location-based hashtags

- Short videos are incredibly popular on Instagram. Create videos that explain the value of being a member, conduct short interviews with members, and reveal what happens behind the scenes.

- Use image styles, fonts and colour to create your brand story. Associations that create a strong brand profile using colours, fonts and filters are instantly recognisable. Users immediately get a feel for what you stand for. Be mindful that most people look at Instagram on their phone, so check that your font and colour selection is clear on a small screen. Have a look at other Instagram accounts to see what types of images work and what colours and fonts stand out.

- Posting behind-the-scenes images makes you instantly more relatable to your audience. People love to see the daily routines of those they follow, as it creates a more personal connection.

- It's quick to create and upload content to Instagram. You can do it from your phone in just a few minutes. Use your camera app to take photos, then edit using the Instagram app or a third-party app such as VSCO, Snapseed or Color Splash. Other apps such as Word Swag allow you to place a text overlay on your image.

- People today expect real-time marketing. Instagram, especially Instagram Stories, allows you to market in this way. Consider using Instagram Stories to tell people what is happening *right now*. Note that Stories disappear after 24 hours, so if you're promoting a long-running activity, you will need to update your story regularly.

LINKEDIN

Like Facebook, LinkedIn allows you to create a company page, individual profiles and groups.

Reasons why associations should consider LinkedIn include:

- It's a great way to get your advocacy work in front of people who can help you effect change.

- It's a recruitment tool. More and more people are turning to LinkedIn to search for a new job.

- LinkedIn InMail is a handy tool to connect with potential members, especially if you don't have their contact details.

- Like Facebook, LinkedIn groups provide a forum for members to engage with each other and have conversations about events, issues and opportunities. LinkedIn groups are easy to set up and manage.

- LinkedIn is a great place to share long-form blog posts and articles, especially if you use hashtags to highlight the topic.

- Advertising and promoted posts can be specifically targeted to geography, industry and role type.

SNAPCHAT

If you are targeting a younger demographic (30 years and under), then you need to consider using Snapchat. Snapchat is fun to use. It's a great way to share images and video, however, it is not going to be the social networking channel of choice for most associations.

Reasons to consider using Snapchat include:

- Most of its users are aged under 25 years.

- It allows you to quickly tell stories to an engaged audience.

- You can use it to easily share promotions – simply snap a code and link it to the relevant website URL.

- There is great creative potential to tell a story over multiple snaps.

- Users are engaged for the whole of your story.

- Use Snapchat to augment your other social media channels – e.g. promote your snaps via the other channels you use.

- You can create location-based content and use On Demand Geofilters[8], which allows Snapchatters at your event or location to send your message to their friends.

BLOGGING

I'm a huge advocate of blogging for business, as there are so many benefits for your organisation. Some of these include:

- Sharing your knowledge via a blog positions you as an expert and industry leader. This can lead to valuable media opportunities. It also sharpens your organisational focus by forcing you to think about your core messages.

- Blogging is an easy way to share the latest industry trends, answer your members' burning questions, discuss what's new in your association, introduce your team, share your core values and much more.

- Regularly creating and sharing new content on your website improves your domain authority, Google ranking and search engine optimisation (SEO).

---

8 Snapchat. https://www.snapchat.com/l/en-gb/on-demand/ (accessed 13 November, 2017).

- Sharing your blogs via social media drives traffic to your website.

- Sharing valuable information on a blog can help you reach potential members.

- Your blogs can help job seekers discover the benefits of working for your organisation and provide potential sponsors and partners with reasons to work with you.

TIPS FOR CREATING A BLOG

- Have a clear idea of what you want your blog to achieve. Do you want it to raise awareness of your association? Do you want it to encourage a change in behaviour? Do you want to use it to get to know your community better?

- Write a plan for your blog and set some goals. How often will you blog? The frequency isn't important, but consistency is.

- Work out your approval process. If you have a team of writers, set editorial guidelines around what is acceptable (for example, in terms of language used). Decide who will have the final say on what is posted and who will respond to comments.

- Prepare an editorial calendar. Work out who will write about what and when and establish a schedule. This will ensure a level of consistency and help you work out what the association will blog about.

- Ask your readers (via Twitter, Facebook, your newsletter, etc.) what they would like to read about.

- Keep your ideas in a central place – a paper file, the notes app on your phone or an Evernote account.

- Read other blogs to stimulate ideas.

- Link posts back to other posts you have written (this is good for your website SEO).

- Block out a regular time to write.

- Promote your blog on your social media accounts.

PODCASTING

Podcasting is a growing medium. Organisations are increasingly discovering that podcasting offers numerous benefits, including:

- You have a greater chance of becoming a market or industry leader in this space because few associations are podcasting.

- You create personal connections. Having your voice in someone's ear is intimate. This speeds up the process of your audience getting to know, like and trust you. It's also an effective way of developing influential relationships with the guests you have on your podcast.

- Podcasting connects real people. It's harder to fake sincerity when you're speaking to someone (compared to the written word).

- Podcasting can increase your website traffic, especially if you have a call to action at the end of each episode.

- It can lead to other business opportunities – such as speaking, publishing and invitations to be a guest on other podcasts.

- It increases your verbal communication skills. If you have an interview-style podcast, it also strengthens your listening and interview skills.

- Podcasts are convenient to consume. Most people who listen to podcasts do so while doing something else (such as exercise, driving or housework). This makes it an efficient, easily accessible form of communication.

- It's a low-cost option. All you need is a smartphone, but if you have a few more dollars to spend, a microphone will make a big difference to sound quality – without breaking the bank.

SOCIAL MEDIA ADVERTISING

There are few instances where I would recommend a member-based organisation use any form of social media advertising, such as Facebook Ads. You are a member organisation and you should be encouraging *your members* to promote your posts. If they aren't, you need to take a good look at why that is.

Jay Baer says the goal of social media is to turn customers into a volunteer marketing army. If you are a member-based organisation, this needs to be a priority.

Times when you could consider using social media advertising include when you are recruiting and using ads on LinkedIn, or when you are running a specific campaign (such as promoting an event). Have clear goals and objectives, and know what you want the ads to achieve. Make sure each ad has a clear call to action and is specifically targeted to suit your demographic and geographic segments. The key is to really hone in on who you want to reach.

Consider using video as well as text and images in your ads. Don't just run one ad – run a few and experiment to see which ones give you the biggest return.

According to Gary Vaynerchuk, Facebook and Instagram advertising offer the biggest bargains in terms of value for money. They have far greater value than Google Ads. If you do undertake social media advertising, make sure you set appropriate measurement metrics so you can track the return on your investment.

SOCIAL MEDIA POLICY

I can't talk about strategic thinking without discussing the importance of a social media policy. Having a social media policy will simultaneously help protect your organisation and encourage staff and members to act as advocates.

Whether you are the only employee or there are 1,000 of you, your association should have a social media policy. It doesn't need to be long or complex, but it does need to spell out what is and is not acceptable in terms of language, images and content.

Membership expert Kriti Colless[9], who has held senior roles at various associations, says: "Creating a social media policy for staff is crucial. It gives them a sense of confidence while helping them understand the rules of the game."

Good social media policies are broken into two parts. The first relates to corporate accounts: who is responsible, what type of content is acceptable and what is not acceptable. The second part relates to what your staff (and possibly your members) can and can't say about your association on their private social media accounts, and on the internet more broadly.

It's safe to assume that the majority, if not all, of your staff use some form of social media – such as a personal Facebook, Twitter or Instagram account. They may even blog, vlog (video blog) or podcast.

A clearly set-out social media policy, linked to your code of conduct, will help protect your reputation and reduce the risk of costly mistakes. Set the intent of your policy at the start. Take this excerpt from C&K's social media policy as an example:

---

9 www.linkedin.com/in/kriti

The intention of this policy is to establish a culture of openness, trust and integrity in our online activities, inform stakeholders of their responsibilities when using social media both in a professional and personal capacity and to manage associated risks with the use of new media tools.

Again, your social media policy doesn't need to be long or sophisticated, but consider including the following:

- Specify who can authorise the creation of new accounts and who is authorised to use the accounts.

- Guidelines around engagement, including acceptable content and language.

- What staff can share about your organisation on their personal accounts – e.g. publicly available information, job opportunities and public events.

- What staff should *not* share on their personal accounts – e.g. financial information and criticism of other staff/management/organisations.

- What is considered reasonable and unreasonable use.

- Who manages the company social media accounts and who to contact if you see someone talking about your business online (good or bad).

- Privacy and confidentiality, including when you can use images of people.

- Information security.

- Definitions of harassment, bullying and offensive material.

- Consequences of a breach of policy.

The simpler you keep your social media policy, the better. After all, no one likes reading long and boring policies!

You'll find many examples of social media policies online. A few good ones to start with are:

- NSW Game Fishing Association (for members): www.nswg-fa.com.au/rules.php?Media-Policy-Social-Media-Policy-1

- Football NSW (for members): footballnsw.com.au/media/social-media-policy

- Australian Association of Gerontology (for staff): www.aag.asn.au/documents/item/104

- Australian Association of Social Workers (for staff): www.aasw.asn.au/news-media/social-media

QUESTIONS FOR YOU TO CONSIDER

1. What are your social media objectives?

_____

_____

_____

_____

2. Are there particular people or groups you want to connect with?

_____

_____

_____

_____

3. Where do your members and potential members spend time on social media?

_____

_____

_____

_____

4. What are the demographics of your current members versus your potential members?

_____

_____

_____

5. What type of content will best share your association news?

_____

_____

_____

_____

6. What resources can you allocate?

_____

_____

_____

_____

7. What are the three big things happening in your external environment right now?

_____

_____

_____

_____

_____

8. What impact will they have on your association, your sector and your members?

_____

_____

_____

_____

_____

9. How can you shape your day/week/month to allow time to think and reflect?

_____

_____

_____

_____

10. What does value look like for your members?

_____

_____

_____

_____

11. Is your CEO or board chair open to having their own social media accounts?

_____

_____

_____

_____

12. Which social media channels do you think are best suited to your association? Why?

_____

_____

_____

_____

MEL KETTLE

CHAPTER 3

KEY SKILL 2: CUSTOMER-SERVICE FOCUSED

"Social media is more about sociology and psychology than technology."
– Brian Solis

Managing the customer – your member and potential member – is the most important of the 3Cs for successful social media. You need to know their problems so you can provide a solution. And you need to know their communication preferences so you can reach them on the channels they use.

There are many ways to identify your members' problems. The old way was to conduct research using surveys and focus groups. You can still do this, but these days many people also share their problems on social media. So, it's important you're listening – and asking the right questions.

To create truly valuable content for your audience, you need to know who they are and what their pain points are. Social media makes this easy, as people tend to share their problems, challenges and frustrations using various social media channels.

Do you know your members' social media handles and do you follow them? Do you have a public Twitter list of your members? Have you created Facebook or LinkedIn groups that members can join? These are excellent forums for you to engage and ask questions, and, more importantly, to *listen*.

There are eight steps to being heard by, and connecting with, your members using social media:

1. HAVE A PRESENCE

Now, this may sound obvious, but there are plenty of associations with social media accounts that lie dormant. Even more have no social media presence at all. In this digital age, your members expect you to have a social media presence – especially your Millennial members.

2. BE MOBILE AWARE

Technology is rapidly changing. The advent of the smartphone is one of the biggest game changers in recent years. As Gary Vaynerchuk says, we are living our lives through our mobile phones. If you are not yet accepting of this and failing to communicate with your audience via these devices, you are missing countless opportunities.

We use our phones for shopping, social media, to search for information (often about what we want to buy), to listen to music, to create and watch videos, to take photos, to get directions. Occasionally we even use it to make a phone call.

People look at their mobile phones more than 1,500 times

a week, or 177 minutes a day.[1] It's vital your content is mobile responsive. Women especially are embracing new technology. This is regardless of whether they are employees, business owners or stay-at-home mums. Women today juggle countless responsibilities: work, family, friends, volunteering and everything in between. Yet they still find the time to use social media, up to 10 hours a week on Facebook alone[2], and mostly via the Facebook app on their phones. What this means is if you want to engage your female members, you need to use social media, and you need to be aware of what it looks like on a small screen.

Have a play with your social media posts to see how they stand out on a small screen. Look at what types of images work. What colours stand out? What fonts stand out? Scroll through your Facebook, Twitter and Instagram feeds on your mobile phone and take note of what grabs attention and why versus what blends in.

3. HAVE A PLAN

Write a social media strategy (Chapter 2 outlines how to do this) that dovetails into your marketing strategy and business plan. And then create a content plan (see Chapter 4 for how to do this). This should outline your key messages, where you will share them, when you will share them, who is responsible, and how you will measure success.

4. KNOW THE PROBLEMS YOUR AUDIENCE IS TRYING TO SOLVE AND OFFER THEM SOLUTIONS

Social media provides an excellent opportunity for you to gain

---

1 Solis, Brian. "How to create experiences that inspire people to share." Presentation at Social Media Marketing World, 17-19 April, 2016, San Diego, USA.

2 Sensis Pty Ltd. *Sensis Social Media Report 2017*, Melbourne, 2017. https://www.sensis.com.au/socialmediareport (accessed 25 October, 2017).

insights into what your members like and dislike, their problems and challenges. Connect with your members on as many social media channels as possible. It is particularly easy to follow your members on Twitter and Instagram, and encourage your senior leaders to connect with your members on LinkedIn.

I recently did a quick audit of six organisations I'm a member of, including Professional Speakers Australia, International Association of Business Communicators, Bupa and a credit union. Disappointingly, many of them don't follow me, but worse, they don't appear to follow many (if any) of their members. Talk about an opportunity lost! Especially for my credit union, which missed a massive opportunity to gain more of my business when I recently had a Twitter rant about a bank I do a lot of business with. I would have been tempted to transfer some of this over to my credit union had it shown empathy and asked for my business.

Take the time to listen to what your members are saying on social media, ask them questions and show empathy when they have issues. Create content that provides useful and practical solutions to their problems and challenges.

Look at Uber. It solves many problems taxi companies don't: trying to find a cab when you're out; drivers who struggle to find where you are; not having cash to pay the fare. Uber's solution to all these problems was to create a phone app that helps you find transport when you need it. It securely stores your credit card details and automatically charges you at the end of your ride.

What problems do your members turn to you to solve? If you're not solving them, don't be surprised if other organisations are created to replace you.

In July 2017, Hungarian swimmer and Olympic champion Katinka

Hosszu established the Global Association of Professional Swimmers (GAPS). The aim of GAPS is to give athletes more say in how the sport is run and a greater share of the profits, especially from global events that draw millions of viewers. In a statement, GAPS says: "We believe that athletes are essential to a successful sport. Athletes should have a say in how their sport is formed and how the rules are changed. Right now, our sport's leaders are not involving us in these rule changes."[3]

I asked an association recently what its members' problems were. The CEO told me they complained about the price of membership. Um, no. That's not a member problem, that's an association problem. In this example, the biggest challenges faced by members included keeping on top of technology changes and ensuring exemplary safety standards.

Think about your members. If they are business owners, their main concerns will be cash flow, staff and generating enough business to keep afloat. Give them content that helps in these areas.

The Pharmacy Guild does this particularly well. Its membership comprises community pharmacies, many of which are small businesses. As well as providing its members with information on medication management and primary health care services, it provides a significant amount of business support to help members gain an understanding of potential revenue-generating options, business and management models, technology and IT, community engagement, leadership and resilience. I have spoken at a few of its conferences on topics including social media, communication and marketing, and have always been impressed by the depth of the business stream and the popularity of these

---

3 AAP. "New pro swimmers' association formed", *SBS*, 4 July, 2017. http://www.sbs.com.au/news/article/2017/07/04/new-pro-swimmers-association-formed (accessed 16 November, 2017).

sessions. It shows it knows what its members want, and it provides what they ask for.

5. CREATE EXPERIENCES THAT WILL SURPRISE AND DELIGHT YOUR MEMBERS

Remember in Chapter 1 when I talked about the social media value ladder? I reminded you how people do business with people they know, like and trust, and the best way to build trust is to have conversations, build relationships and create a community.

Doing these three things will help you create experiences that make your members want to renew. Social media wasn't designed as a sales tool; it was designed for conversation and customer service, yet it can certainly have a positive flow-on effect on your bottom line.

Wendy Harman, former Director of Social Strategy at the American Red Cross, says: "Every time I see a non-profit or company using social tools, my brain reminds me that there's no such being as non-profits and companies – there's only a network of people doing work under the same name with the same goals. Social media belongs to real humans doing a very human activity – connecting with one another over shared interests. We're honored that our mission can serve as a shared interest and that our community allows us to be part of their conversations and activities. In turn, our goal as an entity is to provide value and to empower people to get help and give help with these tools."[4]

If you follow this philosophy, you will be well on your way to creating an engaged and thriving community.

---

4 Harman, W. "The Story Behind Red Cross's Twitter Faux Pas", *Tactical Philanthropy*, 25 February, 2011. http://www.tacticalphilanthropy.com/2011/02/the-story-behind-red-crosss-twitter-faux-pas/

Women especially like to use social media to engage. Community is important to us, so start a conversation. Ask questions. Share the stories and experiences of the people involved in your association – the funny, the silly and the embarrassing (with permission, obviously). Authentic experiences help others relate to you, which increases the trust factor.

Do something unexpected to surprise and delight your members. For example, General Electric (GE) ran a campaign[5] a few years ago called #HealthyShare, to coincide with the launch of its Healthy Share Facebook App. The corporation had a shared commitment to creating better health for more people. A key objective was to encourage people to adopt healthier habits, so it created a campaign to surprise and delight customers with relevant initiatives that would help them with their health.

GE set a target to collect 100 addresses a day from its followers and customers, who would then get sent one of four surprises in the post (yoga mats, a basketball, a water bottle and a box of nuts). Each of these surprises was designed to be shared. GE didn't send just one yoga mat, it sent two, because doing yoga by yourself can be a bit boring – yoga with a friend is a lot more fun. The campaign surprised and delighted many people, and generated a lot of positive goodwill towards the company. While this campaign would have taken considerable time and money to coordinate, it increased awareness of the brand and research showed it significantly improved what people thought of GE.

Key to the campaign's success was how it linked closely to GE's core value of creating better health for more people. It selected gifts that allowed it to easily start a health conversation with its audience.

---

5 Lombardo, J. "Surprise and Delight @GeneralElectric", *SocialMedia.org*, 12 September, 2012. https://www.slideshare.net/socialmediaorg/bw21-ny-presentationge?qid=13145eda-7a74-4c1b-b03c-92180e1d47a3&v=&b=&from_search=1 (accessed 14 November, 2017).

Think about how you could run a similar member-based campaign using the resources at your disposal. How can you surprise and delight your audience while linking to your core values?[6]

6. GIVE VALUE

Be relevant. Enlighten, elevate and enrich your members by educating them, encouraging their involvement and helping them feel part of your community.

As I have mentioned a few times, know the problems and challenges your members face and provide them with information that offers solutions.

---

6 Image: https://twitter.com/generalelectric/status/234028644673130496

Members who don't see value in your association won't renew. They certainly won't encourage their colleagues to join. My friend Susan messaged me recently to ask for advice regarding the renewal of her industry association membership. It went along the lines of, "My membership is up for renewal again and I just don't get any value from it. I feel a bizarre loyalty to stay, even though I have no benefit." A second friend who was a part of this conversation said she had never joined, and Susan's response was, "I don't think you missed out on anything."

Compare this to another experience. A different friend was looking to join Professional Speakers Australia. She asked me for my opinion as she knew I had been a member for many years. I shared my positive experiences with her and outlined the specific value I received – in terms of its programs, my attendance at local events and the national congress, its active use of social media, online and offline networking, informal mentoring, the insurance scheme and more. My friend said, "That's great. You're the fifth person I have asked who has raved about it." Not surprisingly, she joined.

The difference in how these two organisations have made members feel is profound. Both are a similar size and primarily volunteer-run, yet one manages to make its members feel extremely valued and one doesn't.

It shouldn't be difficult to make your members feel appreciated. Simple things go a long way. Follow them on social media. Say hello on Twitter, comment on their Instagram photos, ask them questions in your Facebook group and thank them for their responses. Include important details about them in your member database and send cards to acknowledge important dates and events – for example, the anniversary of when they joined, when they win an industry award, and if they have just had a baby (men and women), written a book, received a promotion.

Show value by responding quickly when your members reach out to you on social media. Not responding is akin to ignoring an email or not returning a phone call – it's one of the quickest ways to make someone feel unvalued. No one expects you to be active on social media 24/7, but they do expect a timely response.

A tip for managing expectations is to include your business hours in your social media bio. For example, Vodafone Australia (@Vodafoneau) says, "We're here to chat from 6am – midnight AEST 7 days a week." This makes it very clear when staff are available for customer enquiries.

Monitoring social media must occur every day. Ideally, you will have someone monitoring your association's social media channels during your business hours, whether they are 9am-5pm or 7am-10pm. Just as you have someone managing the phone lines and email while you're open for business, you should always have someone monitoring and responding to queries and comments on social media. If your social media is only managed part time, expect criticism and complaint, especially if you don't set expectations.

If there's a budget issue and you can only afford to have some-one monitoring your social media for, say, 12 hours a week, then spread those 12 hours over the whole week. For example, have them online two hours a day Monday to Friday and one hour each on Saturday and Sunday. This time could be spread even further with 15-minute chunks throughout the day. It doesn't take long to do a quick check to see if anyone is talking to you and needs to be responded to.

Remember that thanks to mobile technology, social media mon-itoring can be done anywhere. You don't have to be sitting at a desk in an office.

7. ASK YOUR MEMBERS FOR FEEDBACK

People inherently like to feel needed, so ask them for feedback. Your members will also expect to be asked. People give feedback to brands because they want to be a part of the process. Don't expect to only receive negative feedback – most people are happy to give positive feedback, but they usually need to be asked in the first place!

If you do get negative feedback, don't take it as a personal criticism. Instead, look at it as a learning experience and a way to improve how your association operates. Whatever you do, do not ignore negative feedback, as this can damage your reputation and negatively impact loyalty.

Here are some examples of questions to ask your members:

- How can we improve your experience here?
- How could we improve our service?
- What services or products don't we offer that you want?

Asking questions and requesting feedback is an excellent way to engage with your members.

8. BE KIND. BE PATIENT. SHOW EMPATHY. OFFER CREATIVE PROBLEM SOLVING.

Kindness, patience and empathy can be underrated, yet are vital if you wish to be successful when engaging on social media.

Social media is global, so many different people will cross your path – different ages, genders, religions, sexuality, cultures, education levels. Not everyone will like you, many will disagree with you. Listen to your audience with the intent to understand, and show kindness, patience and empathy when you reply to questions, issues and complaints. When digital producer and customer experience manager Dan de Sousa[7] was asked to describe how he defined patience in terms of social media, he replied:

> *"Patience in posting: sometimes the first draft may not be as effective as it felt when mid-typing. In the case of rapid response, I've seen customer names get mixed up, or misspelt, or incomplete sentences.*
>
> *Patience with those customers who post multiple replies: sometimes the initial response doesn't answer all their questions, or the tone could've been miscommunicated, and their reply is hostile. Patience with those people helps me write proactively instead of reactively.*
>
> *Patience with our stakeholders: for example, the corporate affairs team may not agree with your assessment of how to manage a situation, or information required for a product rollout may not have been passed to the community management team before launch.*
>
> *Finally, patience with yourself: everyone makes mistakes. Progression is often slower than we'd like, and it can feel disheartening. Patience with ourselves helps with how creative and confident we might be in our work."*

Aim to establish a culture of kindness, patience and empathy, and you will be well on your way to greater engagement with your members and stakeholders.

Be aware of new research[8] that shows while apologising and showing empathy when problems arise is important, customer

---

7 www.linkedin.com/in/dandesousa

8 "'Sorry' is not enough", *Harvard Business Review*, January-February, 2018. https://hbr.org/2018/01/sorry-is-not-enough (accessed 4 January, 2018).

satisfaction is greater when employees demonstrate how they practically and often creatively try to solve customer problems.

MEMBERSHIP ACROSS THE GENERATIONS

In terms of age, the bulk of association members are Baby Boomers (39%), followed by Generation X (29%), and Millennials and Generation Z (21% combined).

For this book, we will take the years of each generation as:

- Baby Boomers: Born 1946-1964.
- Generation X: Born 1965-1979.
- Millennials: Born 1980-1995.
- Generation Z: Born 1996 and later.

It's important to know the feelings, attitudes and habits of each generation regarding social media, as this will strengthen your social media strategy, help you allocate resources wisely and allow you to take a more personalised approach to creating content. Below is a snapshot of each generation.

BABY BOOMERS

Baby Boomers are often forgotten when it comes to social media. However, 82% have social media accounts[9] and 40% check them daily.[10] Members of this generation tend to mostly use Facebook and are avid consumers of content. Because they tend to scroll

---

9 Lockard, P. "Should you Market to Baby Boomers on Social Media?" *DMN3*, 27 May, 2017. https://www.dmn3.com/dmn3-blog/should-you-market-to-baby-boomers-on-social-media (accessed 8 December, 2017).

10 Sensis Pty Ltd. *Sensis Social Media Report 2017*, Melbourne, 2017. https://www.sensis.com.au/socialmediareport (accessed 25 October, 2017).

at a slower speed than Millennials and Gen Zers, they consume videos and images to a higher degree. Boomers prefer email to instant and private-messaging tools, so continue to provide valuable information via e-newsletters (and encourage them to sign up).

GENERATION X

This generation has embraced Twitter, Facebook, Instagram, Pinterest and LinkedIn. Gen Xers share content frequently, so don't forget to add the occasional call to action that encourages them to share your content. They like and read longer-form blog posts, and are happy to be directed to your website for informational content. Gen Xers also shop online more than any other generation, so consider specific campaigns to this group if you have products to sell – such as books, online courses, etc.

MILLENNIALS

Millennials are the largest living generation. They are also frequent users of social media. By 2020 (in only two years!), they will make up 50% of the workforce.

Millennials tend to be digitally smart. They are often connected to their smartphones and are integral to changing how we communicate today. If you understand their values and preferred communication style, you can leverage their influence.

Facebook is their platform of choice, followed by Instagram and Snapchat. LinkedIn is also popular with Millennials, who see it as a way for them to advance professionally. They prefer social media, chat, email and instant messaging on a 24/7 basis over face-to-face meetings, telephone conversations and 9-to-5 business hours. If the only events you run are in-person and during business hours, you risk alienating a large part of your

Millennial membership. If you're not running virtual meetings or webinars, it's time to seriously consider them.

Millennials are most likely to be engaged by content that entertains via stories, video, infographics, images, video tutorials, how-to posts and lists. Millennials switch their attention between electronic devices up to 27 times an hour, so create flexible content that can easily be used and accessed across multiple media 24/7. Successful content might include a Facebook post that can be consumed in seconds while waiting for a coffee, a top-10 list that can be read in three minutes while commuting, or a longer video or blog post that can be enjoyed in 10 minutes at home. Influencers have a lot of sway with Millennials, so consider how you can use influencers to generate social proof (more on this in a minute).

GENERATION Z

Sometimes, it may seem that this generation is comprised of all young children, but they are starting to enter the workforce, so don't discount them.

This is the first generation of people to have lived their whole lives with the internet, so they are extremely digitally savvy. Almost all of them use social media, especially Instagram, Snapchat and instant-messaging services. Facebook tends to be an afterthought.

Gen Zers have short attention spans, so are unlikely to read the longer-form posts that older generations prefer. Engage with Generation Z by using video, live streaming, short posts and influencers. They respond well to user-generated content, so look at how you can encourage them to create, publish and share content for you.

INFLUENCERS AND SOCIAL PROOF

Who are the influencers in your association and industry? How can you use them to your advantage? Are there members who are happy to speak about their positive experiences with your association?

Generating and sharing social proof through your social networks can increase the influence of your association exponentially.

People are far more likely to trust their peers than trust advertising. Which is why word-of-mouth recommendations from friends and family are extremely influential in decision making. Research by Nielsen shows four in five Australians trust recommendations from someone they already know and three in five trust comments from other online consumers.[11]

So, how can you generate social proof?

- **Ask for customer referrals.**

- **Collect testimonials.** Share them on your website and social media accounts. Don't just ask for written testimonials, ask for video testimonials, too. Social proof is more effective with pictures, so if you are including written testimonials, be sure to ask for a photo.

- **Customer ratings and reviews.** Ask for ratings on your Facebook page and on Google.

The fourth way to generate social proof is to use influencers.

---

11 Perry, M. "It's a Trust Thing: Australians Are Learning to Place More Trust in Digital Advertising", *Nielsen*, 30 November, 2015. http://www.nielsen.com/au/en/insights/news/2015/its-a-trust-thing.html (accessed 14 November, 2017).

There are two types of influencers you can use: your members and non-members.

Firstly, who are your influencer members? How can they be encouraged to talk about you on social media? Membership expert Kriti Colless suggests identifying three or four influential members and teaching them how to use Twitter. That way, they can help you reach external key influencers via Twitter when running campaigns.

If you want to use non-member influencers, you will probably have to pay them (which they should disclose), as you can't expect to use their influence for free. The advantage is they often have significant reach, meaning paying a non-member influencer can be far more cost effective than traditional advertising.

Here are some tips if you are thinking of paying an influencer:

- Make sure the influencer's market is your target market.

- Ask the influencer for their media kit or for a description of their readers/followers. You also want to know how many readers/followers they have – how many unique visits to their website each month versus how many page views.

- Many influencers use multiple social media channels – a blog, Twitter, Facebook, Instagram, Pinterest, etc., which can increase your exposure. Make sure you ask what their social media reach is. How many people follow them on Twitter? Do they have a Facebook page? What are their Pinterest stats? How does their use of social media drive traffic to their website? And how might it drive traffic to yours?

- Be clear with the influencer about what you want them to do and what you will give them in exchange. If you don't have a budget to pay them, let them know upfront. Some influencers will work for no fee, particularly if they are a member of your association, but don't assume they will. That's insulting and it makes you look bad.

When I ran the blogger outreach campaign for Australian Rotary Health's Hat Day campaign, I approached many bloggers directly, as well as via relevant Facebook groups. I targeted bloggers who had previously shared their mental health stories, and who I thought might be interested in being involved in Hat Day.

I was clear in my approach via Facebook and in my subsequent pitch that we weren't paying bloggers (and that I was running the campaign pro-bono). I was equally clear I fully understood if they were unable to participate. The feedback from the bloggers who participated, and even from those who did not, was it was great to have a pitch that gave clarity to these expectations.

- If an influencer does agree to work with you, thank them. Share their content to among your social networks, regardless of whether they are paid. You might think this is obvious, but sadly it's not.

Regardless of the type of influencer you use, make sure they are a good fit for your brand. I still giggle whenever I think of Elle Macpherson's TV commercial for KFC in the mid '90s (check it out if you don't believe me: www.youtube.com/watch?v=G64yu-vIyeSo).

There are various ways associations and influencers can work together. Some of these include:

- Sponsored posts (blog, podcast, video, Instagram, Facebook, etc.).

- Sponsored feature article.

- Giveaway of tickets to an event.

- Mention in a newsletter.

- Mentions on other social media.

- Advertising on a blog.

- Brand ambassadorship.

CUSTOMER SERVICE AND THE MEMBER EXPERIENCE

"Social customer service is a customer spectator sport."
– Jay Baer

There are three main reasons why people turn to social media for customer service:

1. To ask for help with a service issue.

2. To praise a brand for a great experience.

3. To share information about their experience (which could be good or bad).

I spend a lot of time on social media, and I see some very impressive rants about poor customer service. Good customer service is more important now than ever, as research suggests that by 2020, the majority of purchasing decisions will be based on customer experiences instead of traditional marketing.

Is it fair to say customer experience is the new marketing?

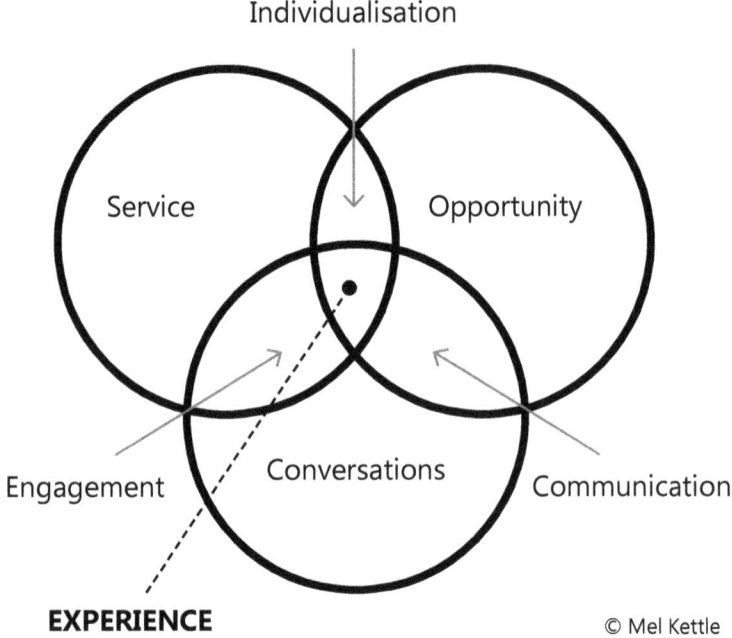

© Mel Kettle

Customer experience is quickly overtaking price and product as the brand differentiator. And providing a positive customer experience is so much more than customer service. It's about looking at how you promote who you are and how you and your organisation build the know, like and trust factor.

There are three ways to give your members a positive experience:

1.   Provide great individualised service.

2.   Have conversations with them.

3.   Provide them with opportunities to interact with you in a positive way, online and offline.

Using customer engagement to create positive customer experiences has many benefits. Research in the *Harvard Business Review*[12] showed organisations that engage positively with their customers have a higher rate of trust, and organisations high in trust report 76% more engagement with their customers. These organisations also have 50% higher productivity and 74% less stress within their workforce.

We need to remember that "perception is reality" and perception is the lens through which people see the world. This includes how they see the service and value they are provided by your association. Look at the value you provide your members. Does this match their perception?

Think back to Chapter 1 when I quoted my friends' experiences with the associations they were members of. I can guarantee when Lisa said, "All the benefits were held in capital cities," that this was not the reality. However, it was her perception. I'm also sure Wendy's association offered a lot more than just a cut-price conference ticket. But again, this was her perception. Which meant it was also her reality.

Where are your opportunities to improve your members' perceptions of what you offer?

---

12 Zak, P. "The Neuroscience of Trust", *Harvard Business Review*, January-February 2017 issue. https://hbr.org/2017/01/the-neuroscience-of-trust

Customer experience expert Shep Hyken says, "There's a big difference between satisfied customers and loyal customers. Satisfaction is a rating, loyalty is an emotion."

My friend Emily (www.dremilyverstege.com)[13], a customer experience futurist, tells this story of the gift she received from a friend: "When my baby was born, she sent me a one-hour massage voucher. And she also offered to send a driver to pick me up and take me there and back. Via the shops. This woman gets that new mums are tense, want time for themselves, have no food in the fridge and are so tired they shouldn't be on the road!"

Emily uses this example a lot to explain why you need to customise the service experience. Know your members, know what makes them tick and provide them with experiences that matter.

The member experience is also important to consider given the increasing use of smartphones to access social media. ALL organisations need to lift their game in terms of service. Otherwise, you could see yourself splashed on the first page of a Google search for all the wrong reasons. Of course, if you don't yet have an active social media presence, you may not even know what is being said until it's too late to do anything about it!

Dan Gingiss, in his book *Winning at Social Customer Care*, says, "If you don't get the offline experience right, you will suffer the consequences in social media."

Who remembers the United Breaks Guitars debacle?[14] It's had

---

13 Emily is awesome. Keep an eye out for her first book on customer experience, due out mid-2018. Sign up to her newsletter (via her website) to find out more. #notsponsored

14 Sawhney, R. "Broken Guitar Has United Playing the Blues to the Tune of $180 Million", *Fast Company*, 30 July, 2009. https://www.fastcompany.com/1320152/broken-guitar-has-united-playing-blues-tune-180-million (accessed 14 November, 2017).

almost 18 million YouTube views and rising. All because United Airlines didn't reply to complaints of poor customer service from a very unhappy customer.

Musician Dave Carroll was flying with United Airlines when he noticed the luggage handlers outside throwing guitars around – and breaking his. He complained to the airline: he tweeted, phoned and wrote, seeking $1,200 compensation to repair his damaged guitar. He would have accepted travel vouchers instead of cash, however, United Airlines refused. After nine months of trying to get compensation, he wrote a song called "United Breaks Guitars". You can watch and listen to it on YouTube: www.youtube.com/watch?v=5YGc4zOqozo

When the video reached 150,000 views, United *then* offered him money to remove the video; not to apologise for breaking his guitar, but because it was unhappy with how it was being portrayed. Not surprisingly, Carroll said no. This incident happened in 2008, yet it still impacts on United's brand image. There were reports at the time that this incident wiped $180 million off United's share price, however, this figure hasn't been substantiated.

Social media gives your members the tools to amplify their experience in a very public way. If you don't have a social media presence, how will you know what is being said? And how will you be able to respond?

BEING AUTHENTIC

*"Communication works best when we combine appropriateness
with authenticity."*
– Sheryl Sandberg

*"Authenticity is a collection of choices that we have to make every
day. It's about the choice to show up and be real. The choice to be
honest. The choice to let our true selves be seen."*
– Brené Brown

It's easier to build a relationship based on trust when you show
your authentic self. This is true regardless of whether you are an
individual or a brand. To start with, it's much harder to put up
a fake front. Being yourself is so much easier! And when you are
authentic, people relate to you.

Remember, people aren't stupid. They know when you're being
fake: your words don't quite ring true, they start to deviate from
your core values. And it's incredibly hard to keep up a pretence,
especially over a long period of time. If you don't believe me,
watch the fakeness get stripped away on the reality show *I'm a
Celebrity, Get Me Out of Here!*[15]

Authenticity consists of four dimensions: continuity, originality,
reliability and naturalness. Here are some ways that you and
your association can demonstrate these:

- **Be real.** Show your true self, whether this is as an
  individual or a brand. Know your values and what you stand
  for and share them.

---

15 Before you question my TV viewing habits, I'm just going to say I have never watched
a whole episode of *I'm a Celebrity, Get Me Out of Here!* I do, however, LOVE *Survivor*.

- **Do what you promise.** If you promise service excellence, then respond to emails, tweets, Facebook messages and other social media mentions. Your customers expect this!

- **Listen to your audience and be responsive.** Don't just talk at them. Engage with them on social media, encourage them to converse with you, and acknowledge and act on criticisms – even if it's just a simple, "Thank you for your feedback." Show empathy.

- **Be honest about your products and services.** If something goes wrong, admit to it. People respect honesty far more than lies and cover ups.

- **If you make a mistake, OWN IT.**

- **Don't use corporate jargon.** Use language your market understands. Check out www.jargonfreefridays.com for ideas on how to de-jargonise your language.

- **Be consistent with your messaging.** Don't say one thing and do another. I spent some time at a company that espoused integrity and trust, yet there was a rampant culture of bullying. Talk about a massive disconnect!

- **Be original.** As author Oscar Wilde said, "Be yourself. Everyone else is already taken."

How do you show authenticity?

TRUST AND AUTHORITY

"People will forget what you said.
People will forget what you did.
But people will never forget how you made them feel."
– Maya Angelou

It's important to remember social media is called *social* media and not *sales* media. It's about being social, not about selling. However, sales will come, because, as I've said before, people do business with people they know, like and trust.

Social media helps you reach a greater number of people in a short amount of time. The most effective way to generate sales – whether "sales" means getting new members, selling tickets to your events, selling books or other products – is to use social media to build and nurture relationships. It makes the sales process flow naturally.

Think about when you do face-to-face networking: you don't try to sell your services to someone you've just met, do you? So why would you do this on social media? To build trust and authority, adopt the following strategies:

- **Have a customer care philosophy.** Creating a great customer experience and triggering positive feelings will set you apart from your competitors and make people want to become members.

- **Exceed the expectations** of your members and potential members.

- **Share your expertise.** Answer questions and share useful content and industry insights – this helps position you as an authority.

- **Share content regularly and consistently.**

- **Talk to your members.** Say hello, introduce yourself, thank them for being a member, ask them questions and ask for their input.

- **Share content your members have created** – blog posts, articles, videos and podcasts.

- **Respond quickly** to questions, comments and feedback, regardless of whether it's positive or negative. How quickly do you respond to social media messages compared to phone and email enquiries? People expect quicker responses via social media.

- **Set response-time expectations.** If you're not going to be online 24/7, say so in your profile.

- **Be helpful.** Make it easy for your members to find what they want.

- **Show your brand personality** and the people behind it. How can your members get to know your team?

- **Join conversations.** If your association plays an advocacy role, share this expertise on social media. Monitor keywords and the accounts of others to find conversations to join.

- **Share valuable content that isn't yours.** Find it by setting Google alert terms, blog feeds, hashtags and BuzzSumo, an online content-research tool. Tag the author when you share their content to build a relationship with them and let others know it's not yours.

- **Actively monitor your social media platforms** for mentions, but don't forget to also monitor the name of your association, products, services and URLs. Tools such as Sprout Social and Hootsuite are good for monitoring different variations of your handle.

- **Take some conversations offline** so you don't breach privacy.

- **Offer support.**

- **Use your own voice.** If multiple people manage an account, say so. Have them sign off with their name when talking to others.

- **Own your mistakes.** Don't try to cover them up.

- **Check for typos** and broken links and fix them.

- **Use live video.**

- **Be transparent.** Nobody expects perfection. Don't get hung up on a negative view – it's how you respond that counts. Negativity adds to credibility, and no response isn't an option – people expect a response.

- Make your brand and your content **about your members**, not about you.

- **Be patient.** Good relationships take time to nurture, whether they are online or offline.

- **HAVE FUN!**

IMPORTANCE OF SAYING THANK YOU

Don't forget to say thank you.

I remember as a child being a bit whiny because Mum made me write a thank you card to my English grandparents for sending me a birthday present. I really, really didn't want to write it, as I had far better things to do – or so I thought. Mum sat me down and gently reminded me that if I didn't say thank you, then: A) How would they know I had received their thoughtful gift? and B) How would they know I was grateful and that I liked it? And, importantly, if I didn't say thank you, maybe they wouldn't send me any more presents. That was the kicker for six-year-old present-loving me!

My mum raised some good points that I have never forgotten. Think about how you felt the last time someone thanked you for doing something for them. Did it give you the warm and fuzzies? Did it make you feel appreciated? Did it make you want to do nice things for them again?

Now, think about the last time you did something for someone and they didn't say thank you. Maybe they didn't show any form of gratitude. Maybe they didn't even acknowledge what you did for them. How did that make you feel?

If you don't show gratitude when people do nice things for you, why would they want to do them again? I'm finding more and more in business that people "forget" to say thank you. It shouldn't be difficult, but apparently for many it is.

When should you say thank you? Remember to show your gratitude when:

- New members join.

- Members refer their friends and colleagues.

- People answer your questions on social media (or elsewhere).

- You are given feedback.

- You get new followers on social media.

- People attend your events.

- People contribute content to your newsletters, magazines and social media accounts.

Don't limit your appreciation to an online thank you. Why not send a handwritten card or pick up the phone? The more you thank people with sincerity, the more they will want to do nice things for you.

I was visiting friends recently and they showed me a handwritten card from their dentist, which said, "Thank you for choosing me to do your dental work." It was the first time they had gone to him, and I can guarantee they will go back.

My favourite example of how saying thank you can turn into an awesome opportunity is when my friend Amanda went to her local PACK & SEND. She said, "Hey, can you help me? This is my problem: I need to send champagne and wine glasses around the country, and quite often they get broken in transit. Do you have a solution so they arrive in the same condition in which they are sent?"

They did.

A couple months later, Amanda emailed them to say thank you for making her look good to her clients by providing such a great service and looking after her product. She told them she hadn't had a single complaint about goods arriving damaged or broken since using them. And they said, "That's an awesome story. Can we use you in an ad?"

Now PACK & SEND has a national advertising campaign (print, radio and social media)[16] promoting Amanda's business. What a win-win!

---

16 https://www.facebook.com/packandsendaus/videos/1110219415775039/ (accessed 14 November, 2017).

QUESTIONS FOR YOU TO CONSIDER

1. How can you improve your member experience?

_____

_____

_____

_____

2. What are three simple ways you can surprise and delight your members?

_____

_____

_____

_____

3. Do you know your members' social media handles and do you follow them?

_____

_____

_____

_____

4. Do you have a public Twitter list of your members that other members can follow?

_____

_____

_____

_____

5. Have you created Facebook or LinkedIn groups that members can join?

_____

_____

_____

6. What problems do your members turn to you to solve?

_____

_____

_____

_____

7. How can you improve the service you provide to members?

_____

_____

_____

_____

8. Who are the influencers in your association and industry?

_____

_____

_____

_____

9. How can you use them to your advantage?

_____

_____

_____

10. What is the generational make up of your association?

_____

_____

_____

_____

11. How can you best use social media to meet their needs?

_____

_____

_____

_____

_____

12. How can you generate social proof?

_____

_____

_____

_____

_____

13. Where are your opportunities to improve your members' perceptions of what you offer?

_____

_____

_____

_____

_____

14. When was the last time you thanked your members?

_____

_____

_____

_____

_____

15. What does your content look like on a mobile phone? How can you improve it?

_____

_____

_____

_____

_____

MEL KETTLE

CHAPTER 4

KEY SKILL 3: CREATIVE MINDSET

"Creativity is intelligence having fun."
– Albert Einstein

I'm going to let you in on a secret. Growing up, I never thought I was creative. I was a quiet, painfully shy child who preferred the company of good books to people. My high-school art teacher (it was compulsory for eight weeks when I was in Year 8) suggested to my parents I choose another subject. Obviously, my love of art history wasn't enough!

What didn't help was that my mother was an extremely talented artist. You name it, she could do it. She was especially talented when it came to fabric and fibres – she won awards for applique, sewing, spinning and weaving. While my father spent far less time on his artistic interests, he was talented at making stained glass in his own designs. Dad was also a whizz at cryptic crosswords – you need a creative brain for that!

My creative potential was bleak. Or so I thought.

Looking back, I realise my creative skills were not ones people immediately thought of. It's true I couldn't draw, paint or sculpt, but I could make up stories. I could bake. I could sing and play the flute – perhaps not exceptionally well, but they were creative activities I loved.

If you too believe you're not creative, don't despair.

Last year, my friend Simone de Haas, an actor, producer and owner of The Speakers' Director, told me: "Creativity is the ability to create something that wasn't there a moment ago."[1] She seriously changed my world – and my belief that I wasn't creative.

Why is having a creative mindset important? If you have a creative mindset, you're more likely to produce creative social media posts. And creative social media posts are more likely to be liked, commented on and shared. Before you post any content, ask yourself: "Does this catch my eye? Is it something I would like, comment on or share?" If the answer is no, then you need to review your content.

Just as I have outlined the ways you can be a more strategic thinker, there are ways you can develop a more creative mindset. Try some of these:

- **Read more.** And not just the type of book you normally read. I'm a massive fan of crime fiction and always have one on the go. When I decided to read more broadly, and especially a lot more non-fiction, I was astounded at the ideas that sparked – especially for blog posts.

---

1 De Haas, S. A Great Recipe for Life podcast, episode #21, 3 October, 2016. https://itunes.apple.com/au/podcast/great-recipe-for-life-podcast/id1112802072 (accessed 4 November, 2017).

- **Meditate.** Not only does meditation reduce stress and help control anxiety, it opens your mind to new ideas. Research shows as little as 10-12 minutes of meditation is enough to boost creativity.[2]

- **Unplug from technology.** This includes your phone, tablet, computer and TV. All at the same time. Yes, really.

- **Take time every day to be more curious.** Elizabeth Gilbert, author of *Big Magic: Creative Living Beyond Fear*, says: "We live in a culture that says 'passion, passion, passion' … but that can be hard to find when you're tired and busy. Instead, ask yourself: 'Is there anything that I'm even 1/8 of a percent curious about?' That idea doesn't have to make you shave your head and change your name and quit your job; it's more like a scavenger hunt, where you're looking for tiny seeds. If you can consistently do that, not just once or twice, but every single day, and be diligent about following your curiosity wherever it leads, you'll find that creative spark."[3]

- **Create something every day.** Maybe you will take (and share) a photo a day, or write 500 words a day, or knit a square a day. What you create can be private or public, work related or just for fun. Set yourself a 30-day creativity challenge – I bet you'll be hooked after 30 days and will want to keep creating! One of my 2018 goals is to bake something once a week – it's a great way to help me be in the moment, especially if I don't want a #bakingdisaster.

---

2 Schootstra, E., Deichmann, D., and Dolgova, E. "Can 10 Minutes of Mediation Make You More Creative?" *Harvard Business Review*, 29 August, 2017. https://hbr.org/2017/08/can-10-minutes-of-meditation-make-you-more-creative (accessed 5 November, 2017).

3 Rousmaniere, D. "No One Is Too Busy to Be Creative", *Harvard Business Review*, 2 December, 2015. https://hbr.org/2015/12/no-one-is-too-busy-to-be-creative (accessed 5 November, 2017).

- **Write every day.** Julia Cameron, in her book *The Artist's Way*, recommends writing "morning pages" to spark creativity and ideas. First thing in the morning, sit down and write three pages of longhand, stream-of-consciousness words. Capture whatever flows through your mind. It might be something profound, or it might be line after line of, "I can't think of what to write" (not necessarily admitting that I have written three pages of that ...). Don't over think what you write, just get the words on paper, day after day. I usually have two pieces of paper – one to write that stream of consciousness, and a second to make an action list of all the tasks I need to do that pop into my mind while I write.

  Kate Billing, co-Founder of boutique leadership development practice Blacksmith (www.blacksmith.co.nz), has used journaling as a personal leadership practice for years. She tells me it has been a huge source of creative ideas. A couple of months ago, she decided to increase the amount of time she journaled for and commit to doing it daily, and combine it with her meditation practice. Kate tells me this significantly shifted the experience and value of both activities. Together, they have helped reduce her stress and allowed creativity to flow more easily. Which is critical, given she often needs to be "creative on demand".

- **Go for a walk.** Walking boosts creative thought as its act encourages ideas to flow freely. Apple co-Founder Steve Jobs was well known for taking walks, and a 2014 Stanford University study found that when people are walking, their creative output increases by an average of 60%.[4]

---

4 Wong, M. "Stanford study finds walking improves creativity", *Stanford News*, 24 April, 2014. https://news.stanford.edu/2014/04/24/walking-vs-sitting-042414/ (accessed 5 November, 2017).

10 IDEAS FOR A 30-DAY CREATIVITY CHALLENGE

Need a creativity boost? Choose one of these activities and do it every day for 30 consecutive days.

1. Take a photo a day.

2. Write morning pages.

3. Shoot a 10-second video every day (use your smart-phone).

4. Meditate.

5. Speak to a stranger.

6. Write a gratitude or thought journal.

7. Send a handwritten card.

8. Bake or cook a new recipe – your co-workers will love you if you share your baking!

9. Draw or paint.

10. Learn a new language.

CREATE CONTENT THAT CUTS THROUGH THE CLUTTER

The average person has an attention span shorter than that of a goldfish, so it's critical you create content that cuts through the clutter.

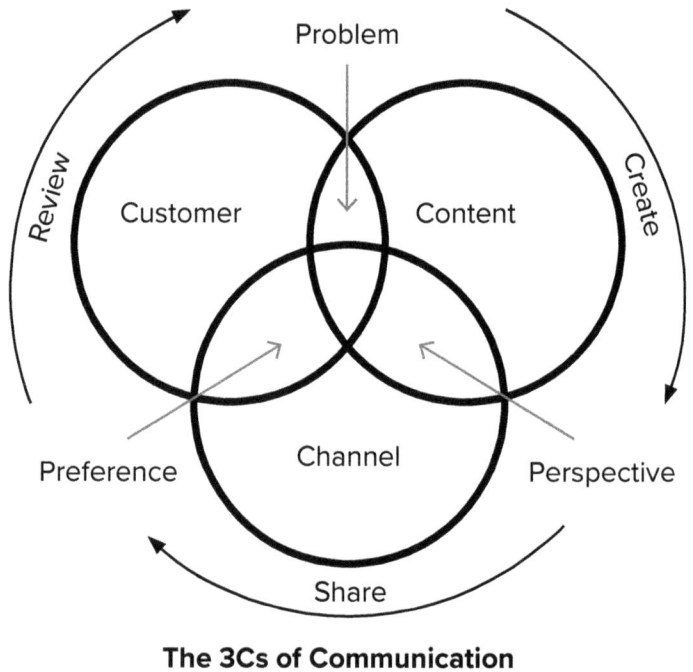

The 3Cs of Communication

© Mel Kettle

Let's look at the content section of the 3Cs model. Content is the currency of social media. The content you share needs to solve your customers' problems. Share your own content, but also curate content – that is, share the work of others. A good rule of thumb is to ensure that 6-7 pieces out of every 10 pieces of content you share belong to someone else (i.e. curated content from thought leaders, members, partners, advocates and influencers). This means that 2-3 pieces should be your original content and one of these can be promotional. Look at your content and see how much of it is promotional versus truly valuable to your audience.

The value of curated content is that it can provide your audience with solutions to their problems while offering them a different perspective to your own. Curating content also saves you time and money and helps strengthen relationships. Sharing other people's content is a generous act; it's like sharing a home-made meal with friends – it improves your relationships and can help people know, like and trust you.

Curated content should be sourced from the websites, blogs and social media channels of other relevant organisations and industry influencers. It can also be user generated. One of the best examples of sharing user-generated content is Tourism and Events Queensland's (TEQ) Instagram account (@Queensland). Every post is curated by people visiting or residing in Queensland. TEQ's bio states: "Tag @Queensland or #thisisqueensland to give us permission to feature your photos."[5] Once TEQ has selected images to use, it contacts the photographer to confirm permission to use their images on @Queensland and its other social channels.

Your audience needs to be at the heart of all the content you share. Yet so many organisations fail to do this. According to entrepreneur and author Joe Pulizzi, "90% of content created in medium to large-sized organisations is about the company, only 10% is audience-centred."[6]

---

5 Tourism and Events Queensland Instagram account. https://www.instagram.com/queensland/ (accessed 7 November, 2017).

6 Pulizzi, Joe. "How to Generate Large Amounts of Revenue From the Content You Create," *Presentation at Social Media Marketing World*, 22-24 March 2017, San Diego, USA.

How do you become the 10%? You need to create and curate content that is valued by your audience. Get back to basics. Write about how being a member of your association can provide benefits in terms of professional development and career progression. If your members are small business owners, give them information that will help them run their businesses more efficiently. Providing valuable content that solves their problems will also help keep you top of mind. If you provide great content, you create opportunities for conversation and engagement, which helps move you up the Social Media Engagement Ladder, thereby building trust.

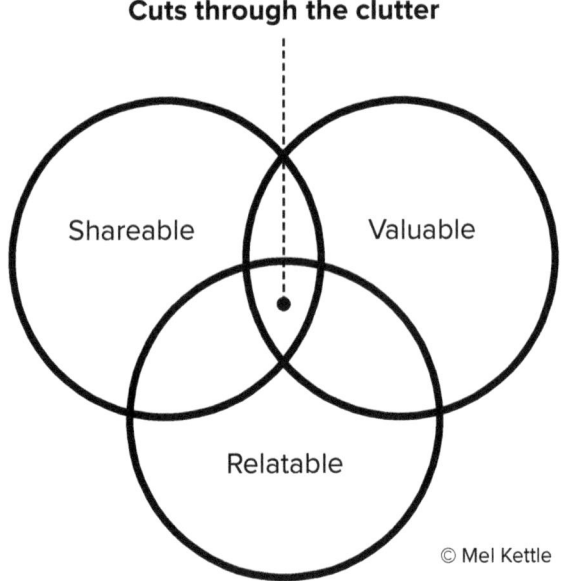

© Mel Kettle

Essentially, your content needs to be valuable, relatable and shareable:

- Give **value** by solving a problem or answering a question. Find out what problems your audience needs solved, and answer them via your content.

- Create **relatable** content by using pictures of real people, sharing real stories and providing real examples.

- Make it easily **shareable**. Content on social media is inherently shareable, but what about content on your blog or website? Make sure you add social sharing buttons to each blog post and page.

You also want to post your content in the right place at the right time. One of the most famous viral social media posts was Oreo's "you can still dunk in the dark" post during the 2013 Super Bowl. All the lights in the stadium went out, so naturally, everyone who was there – as well as the 1 billion people watching globally – turned to social media to find out what was going on. Within minutes, Oreo posted, "You can still dunk in the dark," to Twitter (see image[7] on following page) and Facebook. It was shared more than 20,000 times and reports indicated it was seen by 5.25 billion people – five times the amount of people who watched the game on TV.[8] [9]

---

7 https://twitter.com/Oreo/status/298246571718483968/photo/1

8 Glenn, D. "Dunking in the Dark: the Technology Behind Oreo's Super Bowl Tweet," *Adweek*, 6 February, 2013. http://www.adweek.com/digital/technology-oreo-super-bowl-tweet/

9 Neff, J. "Why P&G's Tide ditched its Super Bowl ad for ... Twitter?" *AdAge*, 4 February, 2014. http://adage.com/article/special-report-super-bowl/p-g-s-tide-spent-super-bowl-talking-ads/291477/

How do we create content that does all these things? We tell stories, we use images, and we create video and audio-based content.

TIPS FOR GENERATING CONTENT IDEAS

If you don't want to create the same type of content all the time, consider these ideas. They can be created as written, video or audio content:

- How-to content that guides people through a problem with specific steps and information.

- Create a list – "The top 10 ways to ..."

- Profile a person (staff or member) or team.

- Show what's happening behind the scenes.

- Develop a case study.

- Do a Q&A-style interview with a member or industry expert.

- Conduct a survey and share the results.

- Share infographics or interesting statistics.

- Create "a day in the life of".

- Explore past events in flashback posts – 10 years ago, 20 years ago or 50 years ago. Highlight how your association or membership has changed.

- Run a photo competition.

- Provide a guide to industry resources.

- Review a relevant book.

- Share awards and recognition.

STORYTELLING

"Marketing is no longer about the stuff you make,
but the stories you tell."
– Seth Godin

Storytelling is essential in business. It's what makes content engaging and relatable. However, the stories you tell must have a purpose. Work out your stories and decide how you can relate them to your work and core messages using images, video and audio.

Well-told stories can make you look smart, funny, insightful and knowledgeable. Use stories to support your association and your brand. Share stories about yourself, your members, your staff and your services or products. Of course, if you're sharing a story that's not yours, make sure you get permission first.

Gabrielle Dolan, in her book *Stories for Work*, says there are four types of stories we need to know how to tell. These are stories of:

1. **Triumph.** Talk about achievements you are proud of. For example, the marketing team winning an award, a successful conference or when a member has a personal or professional victory (make sure you always get permission to share member stories).

2. **Tragedy.** Share stories of regret and genuinely tragic circumstances, some of which might be highly personal.

3. **Tension.** These are stories of conflict driven by your values, loyalties or obligations.

4. **Transition.** Tell stories of change. Introduce the new board

or new staff members, or talk about why you're making operational changes.

If you use these types of stories to share your organisation's values and vision, you will find your members and staff will have a much clearer understanding of what you stand for.

One of my favourite examples of a brand that uses storytelling brilliantly is Saddleback Leather. Look at its website (www.saddlebackleather.com/the-story) to see how it tells its story. It uses images, video and the written word to tell a compelling story that makes you forget Saddleback Leather is a brand selling a product.

Health insurance provider Bupa often shares member stories on its Facebook page (www.facebook.com/BupaAustralia), and images and stories about its team on Instagram (www.instagram.com/bupa).

IMAGES

Most people are visual learners. Research shows people process visual content more quickly than words, and are more likely to remember what they see versus what they read or hear. This isn't surprising, given 65% of the population are visual learners.[10] This means if you use a picture to accompany text, people are more likely to recall what you are saying.

If that isn't incentive enough, posts with images also receive more likes and shares. Ideally, you want to take and use your own photos, as these will be unique to you. It is frustrating to see the same stock images EVERYWHERE! Taking your own photos means this won't happen! One of my favourite examples

10 Medina, J. "Brain Rule Rundown", *Brain Rules*. http://www.brainrules.net/vision

of an association using its own images is C&K. Have a look at its Facebook page (www.facebook.com/candkqld) to see some great examples of image and video use.

If you're not using your own images, don't be tempted to rip an image off Google Images as this is illegal. And yes, people have been fined. A mate told me recently he was fined $5,000 by Getty Images for using a picture he hadn't paid for. And blogger Chrystie was fined $US7,500![11] Use a royalty-free image library – there are many free and paid options.

Consider forming a valued partnership agreement with a stock image library. An example of this is the arrangement Professional Speakers Australia has with Shutterstock to provide its members with free access to images. Is this something that might be of relevance or interest to your members?

---

11 Chrystie. "The $7,500 Blogging Mistake That Every Blogger Needs to Avoid!" *Living for Naptime*, 7 January, 2016. http://www.livingfornaptime.com/starting-a-blog/blogging-mistakes-to-avoid/ (accessed 6 November, 2017).

ROYALTY-FREE IMAGE LIBRARIES:

- Shutterstock (www.shutterstock.com)

- istockphoto (www.istockphoto.com)

- Unsplash (www.unsplash.com)

- Pixabay (www.pixabay.com)

- Pexels (www.pexels.com)

- In 2016, the New York Public Library* released a huge digital image collection for use royalty free (www.nypl.org).

- The British Library recently made more than 1 million images available via Flickr (www.flickr.com/photos/britishlibrary).

Tourist tip: The New York Public Library was one of my favourite places to visit on a recent trip to NYC. It has fantastic free tours, AND you can see the stuffed toys that inspired Winnie the Pooh in its Children's Library.

If you include images of people in your social media content, make sure you have their permission to share the photos publicly. This is especially important if you want to share images of children.

Don't forget to take good-quality images for the "about us" section of your website. Consider hiring a professional photographer once a year to take photos of your team members so there is a consistent look and feel across the images. These photos can also be used for your team's LinkedIn profiles.

You don't have to limit your images to photos, either – use

infographics, drawings and cartoons. If you need support to make gorgeous images or infographics for your social media posts or blogs, check out online options such as Canva (www.canva.com) or Easil (www.easil.com). These two sites have many templates to choose from, and you can create your own images using their royalty-free image libraries or by uploading your own photos. One of the things I love most about Canva and Easil is that they are Australian.

There are also phone apps you can use for image creation. They allow you to either use a stock image from within the app or an image from your camera roll. Some options include:

- Canva (only iOS at this stage).
- Word Swag.
- A Beautiful Mess.

VIDEO

> *"Online video is the quickest shortcut to building your audience."*
> *– Joel Comm*

Cat memes might get the clicks, but they won't win you the business. Video is one of the best and most creative ways to get your message across to your audience. But you need to be strategic with your use of video. A good content-marketing video will show people who you are and what you value.

By 2019, video will be the driving factor behind 85% of search traffic.[12] And if you are trying to explain something to your

---

[12] "Cisco Visual Networking Index: Forecast and Methodology, 2016-21", *Cisco*, 6 June, 2017. https://www.cisco.com/c/en/us/solutions/collateral/service-provider/visual-networking-index-vni/complete-white-paper-c11-481360.html

audience, video is ideal: four times more people would rather watch an explanation than read it.

You can create live video via Facebook, Instagram and YouTube. If you're wondering how to get more reach on Facebook without paying for ads, then you need to use Facebook Live. The Facebook algorithm currently favours posts using Facebook Live (and, to a lesser extent, pre-recorded video), pushing them to the top of the feed. This is particularly important given most organic Facebook posts are seen by only 2% of people who like your page.

Video is an excellent way to help build trust as it gives people access to you, which means they get to know you better. It's also an excellent way to show authenticity, especially when you use live video such as Facebook Live or Instagram Stories.

If you're anxious about putting your face on video, try not to be. Remember that video isn't about you, it's about your audience. However, if you're scared of getting in front of the camera, pretend you're on a video call to someone you love.

The good news is most people don't expect live video to be fancy or scripted or beautifully presented. Do it when you have something to say and don't worry as much about what you look like.

Video is an increasingly valuable business communication tool, but it doesn't need to be complex or expensive. All you need is a smartphone and some basic pieces of equipment, listed on the following pages.

CHAPTER 4

HOW TO RECORD VIDEO ON YOUR SMARTPHONE

Thanks to advances in smartphone technology, it's simple to record high-quality videos without spending big bucks on camera equipment. Here's how you do it:

- Use a tripod to hold your phone so you don't get the wobbles.

- Position the phone so it films in landscape (horizontally).

- Use a lapel microphone (see equipment list below) so the sound quality is as good as it can be.

- Make sure you have good lighting and can see your face clearly on your phone. If you're not sure, record a quick test and play it back to check.

- Choose a recording area that isn't too noisy. If, like me, you live in a flight path that is constantly noisy regardless of whether every door and window is closed, you might need to get used to a lot of stop/start and become adept at editing chunks out!

- If you're doing live video, make sure you have a strong internet connection that won't drop out.

- Prepare your content in advance, but don't script it – it's far more natural if you speak "off the cuff", but use a few dot points to guide you.

- Put your phone in "do not disturb" mode so you don't get any unwanted phone calls while filming!

Continued next page ...

... From previous page

- Give the camera lens on your phone a quick clean to remove any finger smudges.

- Make sure you have enough space on your phone to record.

- Record a short test video to make sure everything is working. There is nothing more frustrating than finding out after your 30-minute video that it had a glitch.

RECORDING EQUIPMENT FOR MAKING VIDEOS WITH YOUR PHONE

Hardware:

- A smartphone with the latest updates (I use an iPhone 7).

- A lapel microphone (I use a RODE smartLav+).

- Lapel microphone extension (I use the RODE SC1 TRRS extension cable for smartLav+).

- Tripod (I use a mini tripod and a full-size tripod, and have had both for years. Have a look at what's available on eBay.)

- Bracket mount holder for your phone (I ripped mine off an unused selfie stick someone gave me).

Continued next page ...

... From previous page

Software:

- Use the camera app on your phone to take photos and video.

- There are various editing software options, but when you're just starting out, look at using free software. I use iMovie on my phone (it's Mac and iOS only). If you have an Android, there are many options, such as FilmoraGo and Adobe Premiere Clip. There are plenty of how-to videos on YouTube if you get stuck.

And if you want to see just what you can do on your smartphone, check out this beautiful ad for Bentley: www.youtube.com/watch?v=lyYhMOXIIwU. It was shot on an iPhone and edited on an iPad while still in the car!

AUDIO

Podcasting is a creative and efficient way to share content. It's a growing medium, and more and more organisations are discovering its many advantages.

Podcast listening grew by 23% between 2015 and 2016. The average time spent listening to podcasts is 4 hours and 10 minutes a week, with 12% of listeners consuming more than 10 hours of podcasts a week. Most of us (71%) listen to podcasts on a smartphone, tablet or portable device.[13]

The importance of audio is increasing exponentially. As people are becoming even more time poor, audio allows you to reach them while they are doing other things. For example, many people listen to podcasts while exercising, doing housework, driving or cooking. You can't watch a video or read while doing something else. Consider developing an audio strategy if you don't currently have one.

---

13 "The Infinite Dial," *Edison Research*. http://www.edisonresearch.com/the-infinite-dial-2016/

HOW TO RECORD A PODCAST

Like video, you can also record a podcast using your smartphone. Apps such as Anchor.fm allow you to record and share your podcast directly through the app.

However, if you want something more sophisticated, there are a few options:

- Decide the format of your podcast – will it be one person talking, two or more in conversation or will you have an interview style?

- How will you record it? If it's just you, you can record on your smartphone, use software on your computer or use a portable digital recorder. If you are recording multiple people, will you be in the same room or different places? This impacts the technology you need. See the list on the following pages for technology.

- When you record, choose a space that isn't too loud. I know podcasters who record in their walk-in wardrobe as it's quiet and the clothing helps muffle harsh sounds.

- Use a microphone (see equipment list) to make the sound quality the best it can be.

- Prepare your content in advance, but don't script it – it's far more natural if you speak "off the cuff", but use a few dot points to guide you.

- Make sure you have enough space on your phone/ digital recorder to record and make sure the batteries will last for the whole recording!

Continued next page ...

... From previous page

- Record a short audio test to make sure everything is working and that your audio quality is what you want.

RECORDING EQUIPMENT FOR PODCASTING

Hardware:

- A smartphone with the latest updates (I use an iPhone 7) or a digital recorder, such as a Zoom H1 (entry-level recorder, around $170), Zoom H4n ($370) or Zoom H6 ($600). The H4n and H6 allow you to plug in multiple microphones, which is handy when interviewing multiple people in the same room.

- Microphone. If you're recording on your smartphone, use a lapel microphone (I use a RODE smartLav+, as I have one for video), but the headset that comes with your smartphone is good if you're just starting out and on a budget. If you are using a digital recorder or recording to a computer, consider buying either a condenser or a dynamic microphone. The microphones that were recommended to me for podcasting were the Blue Yeti (condenser) and the Audio-Technica ATR2100 (dynamic). I use the Audio-Technica and it's been great. I am not an audio expert, so I would suggest having a chat with someone with more audio experience to work out what is best for your needs.

- You might also want to use a pop filter, microphone stand and headphones. All these will improve the quality of your audio but aren't essential when first starting out.

Continued next page ...

... From previous page

Software:

- If you're recording on your own using a smartphone, there are a range of apps, including the built-in recording app that comes with your phone.

- I record over Skype when I have a guest and use an Ecamm Recorder ($30 to purchase and download online) on my Mac. On a Windows computer, use MP3 Skype Recorder (free).

- There are various editing software options, but when you're just starting out, look at using free software. On a Mac, you can use GarageBand (which comes with your Mac), however, I personally prefer Audacity (also free for Mac and Windows) as it was easier to work out how to use it. There are plenty of how-to videos on YouTube if you get stuck.

- You will also need to decide where to host your podcast. Options include Libsyn, Whooshkaa, Omny and SoundCloud.

VOICE AND TONE

The difference between voice and tone is this: your voice is your distinct style, and your tone reflects your emotion and mood.

It's like when you hear a song: some singers have distinctive voices that are easy to recognise, regardless of whose song they are singing. I can instantly recognise when Adam Lambert is singing, or Aretha Franklin, or Sia or Joe Cocker. Despite their distinctive voices, their tone can be quite different depending on the song. Have a listen to Aretha Franklin singing "Respect", then listen to her singing "Tracks of My Tears". The sound – the tone – is completely different: one is uplifting and the other filled with sadness.

The tricky part about written content is that the tone is open to interpretation. If you're in a bad mood, then you probably won't respond well to – or even necessarily understand – a jokey reply to what you consider a serious matter. It will just annoy you! Therefore, it is important to develop a consistent voice.

You also need to teach your community managers the importance of using a tone relevant to the situation. If you get this right, you are well on your way to creating trust, building confidence and enhancing the experience people have when they interact with your organisation.

The voice you use helps create the impression you want people to have of your organisation. Allow your brand personality to come through in what you're saying. Is your voice fun, serious, playful, childish, silly? Friendliness, with a touch of formality, can help build confidence in your organisation.

Your voice is reflected in the type of language you use, as well as the style in which you use it. Do you use industry jargon, acronyms or slang? Do you use a consistent language across your social media posts, website and in your verbal communication? How do you refer to the people who engage with your organisation? Do you call them clients, customers, parents, patients or members?

Many years ago, I was in a meeting with a new client, with about 10 people in the room. I understood probably 30 words in the hour-long meeting because they spoke in acronyms and jargon that was indicative of their business. I wrote notes, and at the end when they asked if anybody had any questions, I put my hand up and said: "Yes, what do these 50 words and acronyms mean? Because I didn't understand any of that." They laughed at me, but someone then had to take the time to explain it all.

I think of this often, as it was such an important lesson about using language your audience understands. If you want to broaden your audience, work in different sectors or work internationally, make sure you use a common language.

Another example I love to share is from when I was an exchange student in Canada many years ago. I was talking to a school friend about something at home in Australia, but she didn't understand most of the words I used as they didn't translate well to Canadian English! I find this language confusion still happens today: when I tweet things like, "It's cold enough for me to be wearing my trakkie daks and uggies," at least one American or Canadian follower asks me to please explain!

You want your voice to be consistent across all your communication, which can be tricky when there are many authors. The best way to create consistency is to have a style guide. I will talk more about this in a moment.

As well as having a consistency of voice and tone in your content, you need to maintain this consistency when you respond to comments and engage on your social media channels and elsewhere. The way you respond is often more tone related and can enhance or diminish the customer experience.

Be aware that writing IN ALL UPPERCASE IS THE EQUIVALENT OF SHOUTING AT SOMEONE. And if you write all in lower case with no punctuation, what message does that send? It indicates you might be a little sloppy, that you don't care much about the way you respond, or that you're rushed. Are these the messages you want to send?

It's also important to know your audience and use a voice that will resonate. New York University (NYU) uses the following voice and tone guidelines in its social media style guide:

> *Who we are: Fun. Witty. Engaged. We value education and revel in belonging to an intellectual community. We believe in looking beyond ourselves and thinking globally. Our next great accomplishment could be right around the corner. We don't know what it means to quit.*

> *Our tone: We are energetic and enthusiastic. We believe in what we do and accept when we make a mistake. We love to converse and enjoy asking questions. We're optimistic but realistic. We tell the truth.*

Follow NYU's social media handles to see how it creates content that reflects its voice and tone: facebook.com/nyu, twitter.com/nyuniversity, instagram.com/nyuniversity.

Some other examples of organisations that use voice and tone exceptionally well are the Queensland Police Service on Facebook (www.facebook.com/QueenslandPolice), the Country Fire Authority on Facebook (www.facebook.com/cfavic) and the

Stroke Foundation on Twitter (twitter.com/strokefdn). These organisations have serious messages, yet they use a combination of serious and light-hearted tone, depending on the message. You need to be able to judge the situation and react accordingly.

It's useful to use the Tone of Voice Continuum[14] to help determine your organisation's tone and when which tone can be used. Consider:

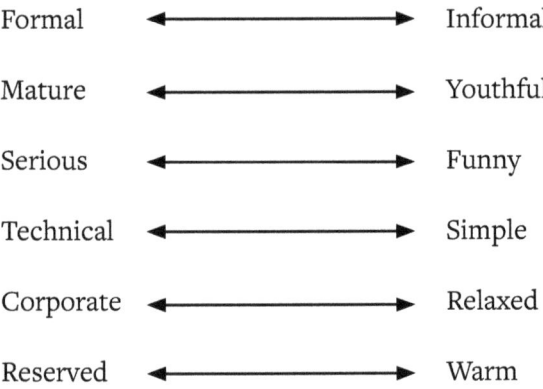

Formal	⟷	Informal
Mature	⟷	Youthful
Serious	⟷	Funny
Technical	⟷	Simple
Corporate	⟷	Relaxed
Reserved	⟷	Warm

Don't forget that a playful, light and relaxed voice won't work for everyone. There will be people in your community who expect you to be mature and serious, and who want a more formal language. While you certainly can't be everything to all people, you do need to be aware that humour and playfulness will not always get your message across to everyone you want to communicate with. Make sure when you do use humour, it's appropriate to the message. If it's a message that needs a more serious voice, then bring that out and set the humour aside.

---

14 Mills, R. "Tone of Voice Continuum", *Robert Mills*, 23 August, 2014. http://www.robertmills.me/continuums (accessed 7 November, 2017).

RE-PURPOSING AND LEVERAGING CONTENT

"Think of it this way. If you bought an expensive pair of shoes, would you show them off once and then hide them away in your closet, never to be seen again? No way! Same goes for your best content. Show it off multiple times, in multiple places, in multiple ways. It's just too good to take it for a spin once!"
– Amy Porterfield

Please don't think each piece of content can only be used once. Creating good content is hard and takes time. Make sure you leverage it to the max!

Let's take that 500-word blog post you have written as an example. As well as posting it on your blog, you can share it at least another 20 ways:

1. Chunk it down into a few different posts (with links back to the original blog post on your website) to share on your Facebook page.

2. Tweet it – with a few different tweets.

3. Share it via your newsletter or magazine.

4. Turn it into a podcast episode.

5. Share it on LinkedIn as a long-form post.

6. Share it on your LinkedIn business page.

7. Share it on the author's personal LinkedIn page.

8. Share it with relevant LinkedIn groups.

9. Share it in relevant Facebook groups.

10. Talk about it on Facebook Live.

11. Talk about it on Instagram Stories.

12. Talk about it on Snapchat.

13. Talk about it in a video.

14. Do a Q&A on video to expand it and share on LinkedIn.

15. Share the video on YouTube.

16. Turn it into a webinar topic.

17. Make a SlideShare presentation.

18. Include it in a conference presentation.

19. Create quotable quotes and overlay them on an image to share on Instagram and Twitter.

20. Make it a chapter or section of a book.

21. Share it on Medium (www.medium.com).

Now when I say share your content in multiple places, I don't mean for you to pop one piece of content into a scheduling tool and tick the boxes for it to automatically cross-post on Facebook, Twitter and LinkedIn all at the same time. This is lazy and boring for your audience, especially for those people who follow you on multiple channels.

It's also important to remember each social media channel has a different purpose and different norms. For example, hashtags are common on Twitter and Instagram, but not on Facebook or LinkedIn.

Instead of cross-posting, look at cross-promoting. This is where you share the same ideas on different channels, but you tailor each piece of content for the channel it will appear on. Yes, it takes more time, but the result is far more pleasing to your audience.

I really like what emerging tech futurist and speaker Brian Fanzo says:

> *"I believe content isn't king. GREAT content is king and brands must focus more on creating great content and getting it in front of the right audience. I 'up-cycle' my content, which means I take one great piece of content and transform it into different types of content for each platform.*
>
> *For example: I record my podcast on Facebook Live, upload audio to iTunes, create a blog post, take four best quotes from the episode and create graphics for Pinterest, take four clips from a month's worth of episodes and create a two-minute video to use as a Twitter video.*
>
> *It takes 30 minutes to record the video and it turns into 6-7 pieces of content."*

WRITING YOUR SOCIAL MEDIA STYLE GUIDE

A social media style guide will be one of your most valuable communication tools. It provides guidance and governance for your social media team. Although creativity is key to creating engaging social media content, a style guide will help your team create and share content that is still consistent with branding, language, formatting and more. To encourage buy-in, ask for input from your whole communication and/or social media team.

As a minimum, you want your style guide to include:

- A list of active social media accounts.

- A description of who your target audience is and details of their personas.

- A description of your voice and tone, with some guidelines to help explain your preferred language. For example:

  - **Clear and simple.** Use easily understood language instead of industry-specific jargon and acronyms.

  - **Conversational and authentic.** Use conversational language as though you are speaking to a friend or colleague rather than formal language.

  - **Honesty.** Instil and inspire trust. If you don't know an answer to a question, tell the person you will find out and get back to them.

- Language and terminology, including: common acronyms that can be abbreviated; upper versus lower case; sentence structure; how to write dates, times and days of the week; words that are not used (with the corresponding correct word – for example, don't say "client", say "customer"); and use of emojis.

- Specific punctuation. For example, do you want a colon or an en dash before an URL? Are you comfortable with repeated punctuation????

- Colour and font palette, and some examples of appropriate use.

- If you take your own photos, include guidelines for getting permission to use images of people (especially children), use of branded elements and any specific styling requirements.

- Ownership of posts. Do you include the name or initials of the poster or not?

- Specific guidelines for each channel you use – Twitter, Facebook, LinkedIn, Instagram, YouTube, Pinterest.

- Examples of best-practice posts for each channel that adhere to your requirements.

- Frequency of posting and guidelines regarding cross-posting and cross-promoting.

- Frequently used hashtags.

- Legal and privacy considerations – these will depend upon your industry.

- Approvals process.

Once you have completed your style guide, link it back to your social media strategy, content plan and social media policy. When incorporated into the onboarding process, it will facilitate a smooth transition for new team members.

There is no point having a well-thought-out style guide if it's unused. Incorporate it into your onboarding process for new staff, and run regular refresher training for your team. If you outsource your social media content creation, it's even more critical that you have a thorough style guide. Take the time to go through it with the people you have outsourced to.

QUESTIONS FOR YOU TO CONSIDER

1. What are three new-to-you ways you can boost your creativity?

_____

_____

_____

_____

2. What are you curious about?

_____

_____

_____

_____

3. Think about content you can curate. What are three sources you can draw upon?

_____

_____

_____

_____

4. How can you improve the content you create?

_____

_____

_____

_____

5. What stories can you tell about your organisation?

_____

_____

_____

_____

6. Where can you source unique images from?

_____

_____

_____

7. What excites you about using video?

_____

_____

_____

_____

8. What voice and tone do you want your organisation to be known for?

_____

_____

_____

9. What Tone of Voice Continuum do you use in your organisation?

_____

_____

_____

10. How do your members relate to it?

_____

_____

_____

_____

11. Write down five ways you can easily repurpose and cross-promote your content.

_____

_____

_____

_____

_____

12. Do you have a written style guide?

_____

_____

_____

_____

MEL KETTLE

CHAPTER 5

KEY SKILL 4:
BE ORGANISED

"For every minute spent organising, an hour is earned."
– Unknown

In Chapter 1, I talked about the reasons why many associations don't use social media. Another common reason I hear is they don't have the time.

Now, that's a reason I question, given too many people (and organisations) waste time doing things that don't add value.

Put your hand up if you do any of the following:

- You procrastinate. This might take the form of procrastibaking* (I did a lot of that while writing this book ...), procrastireading*, procrasticoffee* or procrastifacebook*.[1]

- You don't delegate enough.

- You answer the phone. Every. Single. Time. It. Rings., rather

---

1 These might not be real words, but you get the picture ...

than letting some calls go to voicemail for you to return at a more convenient time.

- You get distracted by the alerts on your phone or computer.

- You feel like you're constantly busy, but you have little to show for it.

- You feel like your day is taken up with meetings, meetings, meetings with little (if any) purpose.

- You feel overwhelmed at work.

- You are a slave to email.

Now, I'm not a productivity expert – far from it. But I do know there are plenty of great resources out there on how to better manage your time so you get stuff done. I used to host a podcast called The Activity Pod (www.theactivitypod.com), which is still on iTunes. My podcast partner Annette Jones and I spoke to lots of highly productive people about how they managed their time. You should check it out.

If you prefer a good book, then have a look at the latest book from my friend Sally Foley-Lewis – *The Productive Leader: How to Achieve More, Reduce Stress and Gain 2 Hours Per Day*. It's packed with great advice.

This chapter is, however, about the importance of being organised when it comes to managing your social media.

SIX MAIN WAYS TO MANAGE YOUR SOCIAL MEDIA TO SAVE TIME AND YOUR SANITY

1. Create editorial and content calendars.
2. Manage approvals.
3. Batch content.
4. Time chunk.
5. Schedule posts.
6. Outsource.

1. CREATE EDITORIAL AND CONTENT CALENDARS

Editorial and content calendars are not quite the same thing, although many people use the terms interchangeably.

An editorial calendar is a high-level plan, usually developed annually, and shared with a wide audience. It reflects your core goals and is linked to your strategic, membership and marketing plans. It highlights overarching activities and themes you need to provide content for, such as a membership drive, renewals campaign, your main events and industry activities relevant to your membership.

Creating an editorial calendar allows you to see key events, core themes, and when you have peaks and troughs. Ideally, you should plan your content a year ahead, but allow room for flexibility, especially if your association or industry is heavily impacted or influenced by external activities outside your control.

A content calendar is a document that tracks your daily or weekly progress of when and how you share your content across various platforms. It will help you plan and schedule your content, so you get the right message to the right audience using the right channels. If you share your editorial calendar across your organisation and let people know you have a plan, strategy, schedule and purpose, then they can more easily identify content that could be relevant and useful to your audience.

A big advantage of having a content calendar is that it helps you save time and can make it easier to say no to colleagues who think they have awesome content but really don't. If somebody comes to you and says, "I've got a fantastic idea for a post," and you think it's awful, then you can say to them, "Thanks very much, but we have a content plan and we're fully booked for the next three months with content. Let me have a look at it and I'll see if I can slide it in." Conversely, if they give you something and you love it, make sure your content plan is flexible enough to fit it in.

Kate Agnew, communications assistant at Dietitian Connection, has a highly structured editorial and content calendar. In October/November each year, she sits down and creates her editorial calendar for the whole of the following year. She also details out the first six months of her content calendar. As a 6,000-strong member-based organisation with only two full-time staff, they need to be organised! A detailed editorial calendar and content calendar helps them streamline their time, so they can maximise their impact and budget.

Before you start your calendars, do an audit of the content you have:

- Are there podcasts, videos or recordings of speeches that can be transcribed and repurposed into blog posts or other videos or podcasts?

- What about slide decks or white papers that can be repurposed into blog posts, videos or podcasts?

- Are there old blog posts that can be updated, refreshed and re-posted?

- Can you interview (audio or video) and transcribe your colleagues talking about their expertise?

- Is there interesting research or data that can be turned into an article or infographic?

- If your association has multiple chapters, what content have your colleagues produced that you can tap into? Can you use it as is or do you need to update or repurpose?

- Do you have good relationships with similar international associations? Do they have relevant content you can access?

Once you have done an audit of your content, review key dates for the year ahead. What external dates are relevant? There are days and weeks for almost everything you can think of, ranging from the serious – such as Mental Health Week, World Cancer Day and World Tourism Day – through to the somewhat more trivial. Apparently, today (14 November) is Pickle Day and Spicy Guacamole Day. If I need to procrastinate at all tomorrow (who am I kidding, I'm on a tight deadline! Of *course* I'll procrastinate!), I'll be completely justified in cleaning out the fridge, as it's Clean Out Your Refrigerator Day! And if your name is Jane Addams, you're in luck – it's your day on 10 December. Now I've started down this rabbit hole I could go on, but instead you should check out www.timeanddate.com/holidays/fun.

For more serious days, have a look at www.australia.gov.au/about-australia/special-dates-and-events.

Once you have audited your content and identified key dates, it's time to create your content calendar.

It's worth taking the time to create a robust content calendar. Yes, they can be arduous to produce, but you will thank yourself for the rest of the year once it's done, as its benefits are many. If you do a Google search, you will find some great templates and tools to help you.

At its simplest, an editorial calendar can be one page divided into 12 boxes, with each box representing the 12 months of the year. Key dates, activities and content ideas are marked in each box. Content calendars are more complex, however, they can easily be created in a spreadsheet with one month per tab, including columns for:

- Topic and title.

- Content type (blog post, whitepaper, podcast, video, etc.).

- Links to supporting documents, such as reference articles.

- Audience segment.

- Organisational values the content relates to.

- Author.

- Date commissioned, due date and publication date/time.

- Related activities or dates, either internal or external (for example, an internal membership campaign or the school holidays).

- Social (and other) channels it will be promoted on and

when. As mentioned in Chapter 4, there are many ways to leverage a piece of content, so make sure you take advantage of them.

If you want to be really sophisticated, you could even colour code your calendar by content, author or core values. You might also want to theme your content – either by day of the week or month. Common theming conventions are Motivational Monday, Throwback Thursday and Fun Friday.

2. MANAGE APPROVALS

Social media works best when it's in real time. This means having a lengthy approvals process often doesn't work well, especially if you are trying to respond quickly. Approvals processes can be problematic, and slow, when there are multiple people involved. However, they are a necessary part of social media management.

There are usually three types of content that need to be approved:

1. Operational or "business as usual" content.
2. Campaign content.
3. Responding to comments.

The easiest way to seek approvals is to get them before you need them. Establish an effective process – who needs to be involved, how much time is needed, what kind of content needs to be approved and what doesn't need to be approved. Consider having a couple of approval timeframes – one for regular content and campaigns (which might take a couple of weeks), and one for urgent matters that need a quick approval turnaround of an hour or less.

An option that can work well is establishing pre-approved protocols for common operational questions. This gives your social team some autonomy and allows for a quick response, which is crucial with social media. If there are questions you are frequently asked, prepare some standardised responses and get them pre-approved. But make sure when you do respond to people, you don't give a "cut-and-paste" response; instead, use language that shows empathy and provides a solution to the problem posed.

Your social media team needs to be aware of your social media policy, protocols and style guide. In terms of responding to comments and questions on your social channels, have clear processes in place that stipulate what can be responded to without individual approval, and what topics might need to be escalated if the matter is potentially sensitive or has legal ramifications.

It's also a great idea to create content in advance for campaigns to allow time for approvals. Approvals can be managed manually or in a more automated way. When I worked in government (about 12 years ago), all approvals for communication campaigns were via a written brief that was printed and passed up the chain of approvals, getting signed by each person. It was a slow and painful process for everyone.

Fortunately, technology today can simplify and speed up this process. A few options for you to consider are:

- Google Docs or Google Sheets. These work well if you don't have a lot of approvals or if you are a small association.
- Rivuu.
- HeyOrca.
- CoSchedule.
- GAIN.

3. BATCH CONTENT

Batching is when you do similar tasks at the same time. For example, when you create a Facebook post, you need to do a series of tasks: write the content, create the image and schedule the post. If you sit down to create and schedule five Facebook posts, and you do these tasks individually and for each post, you expend extra time as you move from the app you write the post in, to the app you create the image in, to the app you schedule in. This process is repeated for each post.

Instead, consider doing this: write your five pieces of content, create your five images, then schedule your five posts. You will save time.

If you create video, block off half a day a month to create three or four videos at once. My friend Dani (www.danivalent.com) creates countless videos for her business. Every couple of months, she hires a video team and shoots five or six videos over the course of a (very long) day. This also means she saves time and money on hair and makeup, as she's not having to re-do them six times over.

Have a think about what other tasks you can batch. I usually batch reading and replying to emails, undertaking research, admin duties (paying bills, returning phone calls), writing content and creating images.

4. TIME CHUNK

While batching means doing like tasks at the same time, time chunking is where you focus on the one single task (ideally, without distraction) before moving on to the next one.

My favourite way to time chunk is to go to a café for an hour.

This has multiple benefits: it gets me out of the office and into a more creative space, I get a little exercise during the day as I usually walk to my local café, and I have a cup of proper coffee. I go with a specific task in mind, which is usually writing related. I set a goal – it could be to write a set number of words or complete a blog post – and I set a time limit of an hour, as I feel guilty if I am there for longer than an hour and only ordering one coffee!

There are many ways to manage your time when time chunking. Two of my favourites are the Pomodoro technique and the 52:17 rule. With the Pomodoro technique, you work for 25 minutes, then have a five-minute break. The 52:17 method is similar, except you work for 52 minutes, then do something non-computer related for 17 minutes.

Both methods are designed to improve your daily productivity by maintaining your focus and creativity. Of course, if you want to be truly productive, make sure you turn off all your phone and computer alerts, log out of your email, don't get distracted by Facebook, and put your phone on silent and in another room.

Tasks that work well with time chunking include:

- Developing a content strategy.

- Creating content – words, images, video and audio.

- Preparing a campaign plan.

- Writing campaign reports.

- Preparing for a meeting.

I'm often asked how often you should spend time on different social media tasks. This table gives you some guidance:

DAILY	WEEKLY	MONTHLY
Respond to comments on your social channels. Check in at least 2-3 times a day.	Schedule all your content for the week ahead.	Schedule all your content for the week ahead. Create 4-5 short videos over a full day.
Comment on other accounts.	Check your stats and see what was most popular.	Do a photo shoot to add to your content library.
Check your newsfeed.	Check your hashtags (Instagram and Twitter).	Remind newsletter subscribers of your social media platforms and to follow/like you.
Monitor hashtags and keywords relevant to your industry.	Analyse the analytics of your social channels and website.	Batch write blog posts.
Respond to comments on your social channels. Check in at least 2-3 times a day. Yes, this is important enough to mention twice!	Find 10 new people to follow/like on each channel.	Record 4-5 podcast episodes.

5. SCHEDULING POSTS

One of the most time-consuming aspects of managing social media is scheduling. In the early days of social media, every post had to be published in the moment, which meant for a somewhat disjointed day.

Today, there are many options for scheduling your social media posts, from in-app options to third-party apps.

The benefits of scheduling your posts are numerous, and include:

- You save a lot of time.

- You achieve posting consistency.

- You can post 24/7 to accommodate different time zones without having to be awake.

- It keeps you visible.

- You can spread the timing of your posts throughout the day, rather than post five pieces of content in five minutes.

- You can be active online when you're doing offline tasks.

There are a few ways you can schedule your posts. You can sit down once a day and schedule posts for that day, or you could do this once a week or once a month. If you post questions, make sure they are scheduled at a time when someone can respond to answers.

Some tools to use for scheduling include:

- SmarterQueue and Meet Edgar. These allow you to create a library of posts that can cycle through your schedule.
- Hootsuite.
- Buffer.
- Sprout Social.

Be careful with using a third-party app for scheduling posts on Facebook, as you may find this impacts your reach. Consider scheduling directly from Facebook instead.

6. OUTSOURCE

Outsourcing is an excellent option if you need extra social media support. The social media tasks that respond well to outsourcing include:

- Developing your social media strategy.
- Content creation: writing, photography, video and graphic design.
- Interpreting your analytics.

Whatever you do, do not outsource your day-to-day social media engagement. You can't outsource your authenticity, nor should you want to. It's like sending someone else on a date with your prospective boyfriend. You just wouldn't.

Be aware there are many people out there promoting themselves as social media "experts". To give you an idea, over the past couple of years I have been approached by accountants, hairdressers, beauticians, cleaners, uni students, nurses and more, asking for my advice on setting up a social media business. None of these people had any understanding of the fundamentals of marketing, and most had little, if any, social media expertise outside of their personal use. They wanted to tap into the "next big thing" and make money from Facebook. It's not that simple.

I'm restraining myself from having a rant; instead, I'm going to give you some guidance on what to look for when outsourcing your social media. These tips also apply when you want to recruit someone for a social media role.

First and foremost, you need to remember social media is a tool that helps with your marketing and customer service. It's a business tool, just as a website, brochure and exhibition booth are business tools. Would you ask someone with minimal expertise to create your website, design your membership collateral or build you an exhibition booth? I'm guessing the answer is no. So, if your "expert" has no experience in marketing, communication or customer service, do you really want them to guide you through your social media?

When choosing someone to outsource aspects of your social media to, find out the following:

- What is their overall marketing and communication experience? Do they have a degree? What is it in? Have they developed marketing communication strategies that include a digital and/or social media component? (A degree isn't necessarily essential, particularly if they have years of experience in marketing communication).

- How would they integrate your social media activity with your other marketing activity? Social media doesn't operate in a vacuum, and Facebook is definitely *not* a strategy.

- What social media tools do they use personally and how do they use them? Do they have conversations on Twitter? Or do they spam people with their opinions? Do they post interesting, relevant content on Facebook and engage with their fans? What does their LinkedIn profile look like? Do they blog and do people comment? What is their Instagram profile like? Do they use Pinterest? Now, I'm not saying all social media consultants or potential employees will have an active personal account on all these platforms, but they should know what they are, how to use them and be using at least two or three regularly in ways that engage with their followers.

- How would they manage your online presence and build your community? Anyone can send a few tweets and schedule some Facebook posts.

- Ask to see examples of content they have created. Is it all written content? How do they incorporate images, video and audio? If you are hiring for a small team, you want them to have multiple skills.

- What sized budgets have they worked with? If you have a microscopic budget, you want someone who knows how to get the most out of that money.

- Who have they worked for? What outcomes have they achieved and how? Ask to see examples of work they have done for other clients, both in your industry and out of it.

- Have they developed a content schedule? Do they know what one is?!

- Do they know the difference between a content strategy and content marketing?

- Make sure they can write, and write clearly and concisely. Social media is often about brevity.

- Do they know rules of grammar, spelling and punctuation? Nothing kills off followers faster than badly written posts.

- What experience have they had in your industry sector? What do they know about your audience? How do they propose to reach them?

As well as outsourcing externally, look at how you can encourage people within your organisation to provide you with content ideas. Once you have finalised your editorial calendar for the year, share it with your colleagues so they have a clear understanding of what you want to achieve. The more people you can encourage to help you create content, the better your workload will be.

However, encouraging others to create content doesn't mean you're giving them permission to post it on your social media channels. You will also need to make sure the content is consistent with your tone and voice, relevant to your core message, and fits with your content schedule.

Consider holding an annual social media strategy information and/or training session. Explain how your colleagues can get involved. You could also provide information on blogging for business and how to use your phone to create a simple video. These are also great opportunities to subtly remind people of your social media policy's guidelines.

ANNUAL TASKS

An annual social media spring clean is a great way to identify what is working regarding your social media, where you can improve and how to streamline processes to save time and energy. Follow these seven steps:

1. REVIEW WHY YOU'RE ONLINE

It's all very well to be Facebooking, tweeting and sharing cute photos on Instagram, but if you don't have a clear reason for being online, you're probably wasting your time. Think about your unique selling point – do you use social media in a way that helps people know what it is?

It's a good idea to have social media goals and objectives so your posting has a purpose. These might include driving traffic to your website, improving customer service or improving brand engagement. Ideally, they will be measurable over time and aligned with your business goals.

How do your online strategies and tactics relate to your offline ones?

2. REVIEW WHAT YOU'RE MEASURING

Work out what you want to measure and set some metrics. Think of these metrics as benchmarks so you can see whether you are achieving your goals. If your goal is to drive traffic to your website, look at the number of visitors coming from your social media channels compared to from other places or from an online search. Which channels drive the most traffic to your website?

If you want to measure the increase in brand engagement, look at the number of people mentioning your brand. How many of these people do you reply to? How many likes, comments and shares are you getting?

There will be more on metrics and analysing data in Chapter 6.

3. DO A QUICK BRAND AUDIT

A quick brand audit should take you about an hour, depending on how many social media platforms you use and how consistent they are. You want to look at your:

- **Avatar/picture.** Ideally, you will be using the same one on every platform. Try to use an image of a person rather than a logo, as people do business with people.

- **Banner image.** Is this consistent with your brand? Did you know you can now use a video as a banner on Facebook? If your avatar is a logo, then make sure your banner image has people and, ideally, people from your business rather than a boring stock image.

- **Bios.** They need to be consistent across your social media, but not necessarily identical. There are different character limits for each platform, so use them wisely. Please also check for typos.

- **URL.** Use the same URL for each social channel or create a landing page for each platform. I like how Nikki Parkinson does this with her Instagram page for Styling You (www.stylingyou.com.au/as-seen-on-styling-you-instagram). Regardless of what you choose, make sure all the links work!

- **Physical address.** If you want people to visit you, include your physical address in the location section. Make it easy for people to find you.

4. LOOK AT YOUR POSTS – ARE THEY GETTING CUT-THROUGH?

Your audience is bombarded with millions of messages a day, so it's not surprising their attention span is shorter than ever. Add to this the fact that most people check their social media on the tiny screen on their phone – it's no wonder it can be difficult for your content to get cut-through!

You need to ensure you're delivering the right content to your audience using the right channels for *them*. It doesn't matter how much you love Snapchat if your audience doesn't use it.

Content that gets cut-through is usually highly visual, uses video or tells a compelling story. Sometimes it's a combination of all three. Look at the language you use, the colours, fonts and style. Do you have a recognisable look and feel? Do you provide content that solves your audience's problems? Do they seek you out or do they pass you by in favour of other, more interesting messages?

Have a good look at what you've posted over the past few months. Does it make you think, "Yes, I'd like, share or comment on that." If it doesn't, then re-evaluate how you create content.

5. REVIEW YOUR AUDIENCE AND ENGAGEMENT

Does your audience engage with you? Do you engage with them? How much social listening are you doing? Do you know what your members' problems and needs are? How can you provide a solution for them? Take the time to get to know them, engage with them and let them know, like and trust you. Then the sales will happen.

6. LOOK AT OTHER ASSOCIATIONS

What are other associations doing on social media, particularly those in your sector? What do their profiles look like? Are they getting more engagement? Creating better content? What can you learn from them?

7. REVIEW YOUR EDITORIAL AND CONTENT CALENDARS

If you don't have an editorial calendar or a content calendar, now is the time to create them. They take a bit of time to set up but will save you *hours* of time in the long run.

QUESTIONS FOR YOU TO CONSIDER

1. Be honest with yourself: how do you waste time? How could you be more productive?

_____

_____

_____

_____

2. What are some of your more common interruptions?

_____

_____

_____

_____

3. What are the key events or activities you can include in your editorial calendar?

_____

_____

_____

_____

4. What content do you currently have that can be leveraged?

_____

_____

_____

_____

5. Who in your organisation needs to approve content before posting it to social media?

_____

_____

_____

6. What are your highest priorities in terms of being more organised?

_____

_____

_____

7. What are three activities you could batch?

_____

_____

_____

_____

8. What are three activities you could time chunk?

_____

_____

_____

9. What are three tasks you could outsource?

_____

_____

_____

10. Who could you outsource them to? Internally or externally?

_____

_____

_____

_____

11. Who else in your organisation could produce content for you?

_____

_____

_____

_____

12. What training might they need?

_____

_____

_____

_____

CHAPTER 6

KEY SKILL 5: AN ABILITY TO ANALYSE

"What's measured improves."
– Peter Drucker

Back in Chapter 1, I told you that using social media will help you achieve your membership KPIs. Elsewhere in this book, I have shown you how to identify your goals, develop strategies, build your profile, create compelling content, be customer focused and demonstrate your value.

The final skill you need to support your communication and social media efforts is the ability to analyse. You need to be able to collect and interpret information, think critically, solve problems and make decisions. You want to be able to measure your return on investment as well as your return on engagement so you have a clear sense that what you are doing is worthwhile.

I'm often asked, "How do I measure the return on investment (ROI) of my social media?" This is often followed by, "I've been using Twitter (or Facebook or Instagram or LinkedIn) for weeks, so why haven't my sales doubled?"

There are two things to be mindful of. The first is that you should focus on both your return on engagement (ROE) as well as your ROI. And secondly, it can take a long time to see your social media use convert into sales.

Remember, too, that social media requires us to be agile and responsive. While we need to have a clear understanding of the numbers, data and analytics, we need to be flexible. Katie Delahaye Paine and Beth Kanter, in their book *Measuring the Networked Nonprofit*, remind us to be data informed, not data driven.

Being data informed is not about being a slave to measurement and key performance indicators. It's about understanding why you capture certain metrics. Knowing your "why" will improve your association's decision-making process and help you reach your goals. Why is it important to know which posts get more likes, comments and shares? Why is it important to understand the types of questions your members ask on Twitter and the frequency with which they are asked? Could the answer suggest your organisation has an operational issue? Or is it not providing information on a topic that is important to members?

In Chapter 1, I talked about how social media is like dating. It takes a while to get to know, like and trust people. Another analogy I like to use is this: you don't set up shop at the back of a public networking event and expect to immediately sell your products or services. You don't expect people who have previously not heard of your association to join. Do you? So why would you expect people to immediately buy from you the first time they see you on social media?

IDENTIFY METRICS TO MEASURE

If you want to have social media analytics success, you must understand what you want to measure. You should have set out your social media goals in your strategy, and these need to be measurable.

Associations use social media for many reasons, including:

- Brand awareness.

- Community and member engagement.

- To share useful content and information.

- Lead generation and sales – for new members, member renewals, conferences, events and other products/services.

- Member support.

- Influencer connections.

Each of these reasons should have a measurable goal attached. These might include:

- **Brand awareness.** The number of followers, the reach of posts and the number of likes, comments, mentions and shares.

- **Community and member engagement.** Measure the number of likes, comments, mentions and shares, as well as the nature of these comments and mentions. Are they supportive, happy, annoyed, etc.? Look at your groups – how engaged are they? If you run Twitter chats, who engages and how?

- **Member experience.** Similar to member engagement, you want to look at the nature of comments and mentions. Are they having positive experiences or negative? What can you do to improve their experience? Be aware that a lot of times people will mention you without tagging you, so make sure you have searches set up for keywords, including your organisation's name.

- **Sharing useful content and information.** This includes the number of click-throughs on social posts, how much traffic to your website comes from social media, and what percentage of traffic comes from social media versus online searches and versus other links.

- **Lead generation and sales.** Look at the number of new members joining and who they are. Also look at the amount and type of sales of events and other products/services you offer. When new members join, ask them how they heard about you. Measure tracking via social ads such as Facebook ads, links to landing pages and email signups.

- **Member support.** How many questions are you asked on social media? What's the nature of the questions? What is your response time? How satisfied are your members with your responses?

- **Influencer connections.** Measure the volume of posts, the reach rates, total engagement, the sum of clicks, likes and re-shares.

The metrics you select should align with your objectives and be used to help you make decisions.

Kate Agnew, from Dietitian Connection, told me that data analytics and metrics are a high priority for her. She spends a significant amount of time reviewing and interpreting this data. Reach and engagement are the two key metrics she measures. Firstly, she looks at the overall engagement score in Facebook Insights, then she looks at the comments, likes, clicks and shares for each post. This helps determine what types of posts and topics are more popular, so Dietitian Connection can create more of them.

She also measures podcast listeners, webinar attendance, click rates and e-newsletter opens. Google Analytics is used to look at the performance of particular sections and pages on their website, and to determine where people navigated to the website from (i.e. from a social media post, a Google search or from somewhere else).

Look beyond the vanity metrics and delve deep into the data. Which social channels give you the highest conversion rates? In my practice, the bulk of the referrals I received for a two-year period came via people who knew me from Twitter. As well as measuring traffic to your website, do you have a process in place to ask people why they contacted you that day? Do you have separate phone numbers linked to your Facebook, Twitter and LinkedIn accounts? Do you use lead pages and have specific calls to action that are measurable?

HOW TO MEASURE YOUR FINANCIAL RETURN ON INVESTMENT

"If you want to measure social media ROI, stop wasting your time doing software demos and attending webinars. Just figure out what you want to track, where you can track it, think about both current customers and new customers, and go do it."
– Jay Baer

Your social media ROI is calculated by subtracting the cost of your investment in social media from the financial return it gives you and dividing it by the cost of your investment. Then multiply by 100 to get the percentage return. The equation looks like this:

$$ROI \% = (R\text{-}I)/I \times 100$$

There are four steps you need to follow to measure your social media ROI:

1. WORK OUT YOUR FINANCIAL GOALS AND WHAT YOU WANT TO MEASURE.

This might include:

- New members.
- Renewing members.
- Registrations for an event.
- New sponsors or partners signing up.

Assign a dollar value to each of these – how much is a new member worth? How much is a renewing member worth?

2. TRACK AND MEASURE YOUR CONVERSIONS

You can track website activity, such as online sales and newsletter signups, via Google Analytics. If you're not sure how to set up Google Analytics, there's a lot of useful information at support.google.com/analytics. Make sure when you set it up that you create goals, a feature within Google Analytics, so you can accurately track the relevant activity.

If you use a scheduling tool such as Buffer, SmarterQueue or Hootsuite, these will track your social interactions, such as likes, comments and shares.

3. DETERMINE YOUR COSTS

Add up all the costs to work out how much using social media costs you. Include your staff costs for their time, the cost of any tools used (such as scheduling, social listening, design, etc.), advertising spend and any outsourced costs.

4. WORK OUT THE ROI

Once you have determined your income and costs, you can measure your ROI using the equation:

$$\text{ROI} \% = (R\text{-}I)/I \times 100$$

One of the benefits of having a good social media strategy in place will become apparent when it is time for member renewals. If your membership team has been working closely with your marketing and social media team, they would have seen the developing relationships with your members on social media. Then, when they call to ask about renewing, the value should be apparent.

Let's take an example. Let's look at a professional association of 3,000 members with an annual membership fee of $800. Every year, it has 80% (or 2,400) renewals. This year, the association decides to have a renewal rate of 88% (2,640 members – an extra 240 members renewing), which will give it an additional income of $192,000. It decides to focus on demonstrating the value of membership and member engagement by using social media (Facebook, LinkedIn and Twitter). Its social media costs are:

- .4FTE of communication officer (salary of $80k pro-rata to .4FTE): **$32,000**

- Annual cost of a scheduling tool such as SmarterQueue: **$600**

- Some targeted social media advertising prior to renewal date: **$10,000**

- Miscellaneous equipment (e.g. microphones for better audio): **$1,000**

Total cost: $43,600

ROI% = $192,000 - $43,600 / $43,600 x 100 = 340% return.

When renewals time comes around, your membership manager (or the outbound call centre, if you outsource) will find it far easier to convert renewing members.

Membership expert Belinda Moore says the decision to join is transactional: "I'll give it a go." Research clearly shows the more actively engaged a member is with your organisation, the more likely they are to renew.[1] Social media is an excellent way to stimulate engagement, which will benefit you when it is time for your members to renew.

---

1 Moore, Belinda. "How to Develop an Effective Membership Strategy," 2016.

TOOLS TO HELP YOU MEASURE

When deciding what to measure, you also need to consider the practicalities of your desired metric. If you don't have the tools or resources, you may need to reconsider.

Fortunately, there are many tools available to help you measure and analyse your social media activities. Scheduling tools such as Buffer, TweetDeck, SmarterQueue and Hootsuite give you access to some data as part of your subscription. Other third-party measurement and analytic products include Sprout Social, Quiip, Meltwater and NUVI.

If you want to measure Twitter and Instagram hashtags (for a campaign or everyday use), look at Hashatit.com or Hashtags.org. Many of these have a free version as well as a paid version.

Google Analytics is one of the best tools around for measuring website analytics, including where the traffic to your website comes from.

If you are a small association or don't have the budget to pay for third-party tools, make sure you review the analytics available for free within your channels of choice. Most social media channels have built-in analytics for business accounts. For example:

- Facebook gives you demographic data, views, likes, reach, engagement, followers, and information per post including clicks, reach, reactions, comments and shares.

- Instagram gives you demographic data, impressions, reach and profile views.

USING DATA TO MAKE DECISIONS

"There is a difference between numbers
and numbers that matter."
– Jeff Bladt and Bob Filbin

One of the first things you need to do if you want to have social media success is to start looking at data. Before sitting down to write your strategy, undertake some research. This should include primary research, such as a member satisfaction survey or conducting a focus group with your members. Find out why they are a member, what they expect from you, and the challenges and problems they have that you can solve.

You will also need to undertake some desk research. Read reports such as the *Sensis Social Media Survey* and the *Membership Marketing Benchmarking Report*. Gain an understanding of the trends in your sector and how they impact your members. Read blogs, listen to podcasts and watch videos created by marketing and social media experts.

Do a SWOT analysis. Look at the strengths, weaknesses, opportunities and threats facing your association. What strengths and opportunities can you capitalise on? What weaknesses and threats must you be aware of and how can you turn them into strengths and opportunities?

Once you have this information, work out what you will do with it. There is no point collecting data if you don't use it to make decisions. Go beyond the basics of looking at likes, comments and shares and leverage the information you have to make more informed decisions for your association. Look also at patterns in the data.

If you are putting a lot of time and effort into Pinterest but it's

not driving any traffic to your website, should you continue to use it?

What types of posts get the most traction? If you create and share one video a week on Facebook but it gets 100 times more engagement than a static post, surely it makes more sense to create more video.

If the long-form post you wrote on LinkedIn about how you mentor young career professionals leads to 20 comments and 10 enquiries from potential members, then perhaps you should write more long-form posts about the benefits for younger members. The data might also tell you the best time to post to reach your audience. Hint: It's probably not Monday-Friday, 9am-5pm.

Have a look at what your colleagues in other associations are doing. Don't only look at associations; look at the not-for-profit sector broadly, as well as member-based businesses such as credit unions, managed funds, health insurers, co-operatives, fitness centres and health clubs. Who is getting great engagement? Who is quickly growing a fan base? Who looks like they are converting to sales more effectively than you? What are they doing to achieve this? What insights can you incorporate into your social media strategy?

One of my favourite accounts to look at is Huggies, which makes disposable nappies. As I am happily childfree, I have never been, and never will be, a Huggies customer, but that doesn't mean I can't appreciate how it manages its social media. It focuses on building relationships with its target market – mainly new mums. Huggies' tweets (@Huggies) are primarily @replies, and often the tweet it replies to doesn't tag Huggies. It creates and follows relevant hashtags, and responds accordingly when people use them.

On Facebook (@HuggiesAU and @Huggies), Huggies runs competitions, shares video, has scheduled live video and shares resources, such as e-books. It creates great content but doesn't overwhelm its audience with multiple posts a day. Instead, it posts new content once or twice a day (if that) to each of its accounts. It has a strong focus on video over written content and creates a lot of content that provides expectant and new mothers with valuable information on how to look after their newborns and themselves. Huggies provides information on getting pregnant, being pregnant and looking after your child from when they are newborn to toddler.

While big corporates such as Huggies will have big marketing budgets, there is still a lot you can learn from looking at and analysing their social media use.

DETERMINE YOUR REPORTING CADENCE

Once you start down the rabbit hole of data analysis, it's easy to want to focus on every single piece of data all the time. And that just isn't practical, or necessary.

Identify how often you need to analyse and report the data, and prioritise it. Some metrics will only need to be reported quarterly or annually, while others are more important to measure in real time.

Allocate some time every week to at least look at your engagement and reach so you can determine any trends or patterns.

SOCIAL LISTENING

Social listening occurs when you monitor social media for mentions of your association, your industry, other associations in your sector, your events and topics relevant to you.

People are always going to be talking about you. Having a social listening strategy allows you to gather insights, generate new content ideas and respond appropriately when people talk about you.

To effectively socially listen, there are a few things you need to consider:

- Determine what you want to know and any social listening goals. For example, do you want more information about a specific member segment? Or do you want to find out what attendees thought about an event?

- Know where the people you want to listen to hang out online. Are they on Twitter, Facebook, Instagram or LinkedIn?

- Know your influencers and where they are.

- What are the main hashtags, trends and search terms you want to focus on? Start with your association name, other associations in your sector, branded hashtags, event hashtags and names of key people (CEO, board members, etc.).

- Identify the tools you can use to help you. Twitter is quite easy, as you can search keywords and hashtags. Other channels are a bit more complex. Some paid tools to check out are BuzzSumo, Hootsuite, Sprout Social and Meltwater.

- What will you do with the information? Have a response process in place for positive and negative mentions.

QUESTIONS FOR YOU TO CONSIDER

1. What metrics are appropriate for you to measure?

_____

_____

_____

_____

2. Is your website linked to Google Analytics?

_____

_____

_____

_____

3. Do you know how to use Google Analytics to get the data that is relevant to you so you can analyse the relevant metrics?

_____

_____

_____

_____

4. What drives the most traffic to your website?

_____

_____

_____

_____

_____

5. What are the most popular pages on your website and on your blog?

_____

_____

_____

_____

6. Which social media channels give you the highest conversion rates in terms of sales?

_____

_____

_____

_____

7. Which social media channels give you the highest rates of engagement per post?

_____

_____

_____

_____

8. Do you have a process in place to ask new enquirers how they heard of you?

_____

_____

_____

_____

9. Do you currently measure your return on investment?

_____

_____

_____

_____

10. What are your financial goals?

_____

_____

_____

_____

_____

11. What do your members expect of you?

_____

_____

_____

_____

12. What do your members value most from your association?

_____

_____

_____

_____

13. What metrics do you want to measure and how frequently?

_____

_____

_____

_____

14. What do you want to report weekly, monthly, quarterly and annually?

_____

_____

_____

_____

15. What do people say about your association and your key people?

_____

_____

_____

_____

MEL KETTLE

FINAL WORDS

I wrote this book because people often say to me, "I know we need to use social media, but I don't know how."

If you have made it this far, you will now know what you need to do to become a social association. Develop your social media strategy, know the value you provide your members, create and share compelling content, have conversations, build relationships, engage with your members and analyse your data.

As you read back in Chapter 1, social media can help your association stand out. Use it to be social, so your members get to know, like and trust you, and you will increase awareness of your organisation, attract new members, increase engagement and retention rates, and create a thriving online community.

It sounds really simple. Because it is. Yes, there is work involved, but it's not rocket science. Just remember the important part of social media is that you are social. Jay Baer reminds us to "focus on how to be social, not on how to do social".

Invest the time to develop your strategies, and make sure to allocate a portion of each day to get to know your members better. The more you know your members, the more likely you are to create and share content they will value.

Don't be afraid to start slowly, with one social media channel. You don't need to be everywhere all at once, and you don't want to be overwhelmed.

If you get stuck, get in touch. Read my blog, sign up to my newsletter, reach out to me on social media.

FINAL WORDS

I'd love to know what you learned and applied from this book. Has it helped you get to know your members more? Are they more engaged with your association? What types of content are you creating? What has resonated most?

Reading this book is the first step to becoming a social association. Now you have the information you need, it's up to you to get started.

I look forward to seeing you online.

REFERENCES AND READING

This list includes some of my favourite books, blogs and podcasts. I hope you enjoy them too.

BOOKS:

- Jay Baer, *Hug Your Haters*
- Lynne Cazaly, *Making Sense*
- Gabrielle Dolan, *Stories for Work*
- Sally Foley-Lewis, *The Productive Leader*
- Elizabeth Gilbert, *Big Magic*
- Dan Gingiss, *Winning at Social Customer Care*
- Valerie Khoo, *Power Stories*
- David Meerman Scott, *The New Rules of Marketing & PR* and *Real-Time Marketing & PR*
- Dan Norris, *Create or Hate*
- Mark W. Schaefer, *Known* (all of Mark's books are great)
- Scott Stratten, *UnMarketing*
- Gary Vaynerchuk – everything he has written, especially *The Thank You Economy* and *Jab, Jab, Jab, Right Hook*

BLOGS AND WEBSITES:

- Jane Anderson – www.janeandersonspeaks.com
- Convince and Convert – www.convinceandconvert.com
- Belinda and Julian Moore, Strategic Management Solutions (SMS) – www.smsonline.net.au
- Social Media Examiner – www.socialmediaexaminer.com
- Dr Emily Verstege – www.dremilyverstege.com

PODCASTS:

- The GaryVee Audio Experience
- Experience This! with Joey Coleman and Dan Gingiss
- Social Media Marketing with Michael Stelzner
- Association Chat
- The Marketing Companion Podcast with Mark Schaefer and Tom Webster
- Become a ProBlogger with Darren Rowse

COOKBOOKS:

In case you feel the need to do some procrasticooking or pro-crastibaking, these are my current favourite (and most used) cookbooks:

- Julie Goodwin, *Homemade Takeaway* – all her books are great
- Hetty McKinnon, *Community* – truly spectacular salads, all vegetarian
- Thomasina Miers, *Mexican Food*
- Jamie Oliver, *Jamie's America*
- Yotam Ottolenghi – all his books are fantastic, however my favourites are *Jerusalem* and *Plenty More*
- Jo Whitton, *Quirky Cooking* and *Life-Changing Food*

CRIME NOVELS:

My favourite crime writers are:

- David Baldacci
- Allison Brennan
- Alafair Burke
- Harlan Coben
- Lisa Gardner
- Laura Griffin
- Karen Robards
- Karen Rose

MEL KETTLE

WANT MORE?

Mel Kettle is a communication and social media expert. She speaks, mentors, runs workshops and facilitates the development of communication and social media strategies, to help associations and other organisations communicate effectively with their members, customers and stakeholders.

She writes a weekly blog and is often featured in magazines and other media. Mel shares her thoughts most weeks via her newsletter, which you can subscribe to at **www.melkettle.com/signup**.

If you would like help with your communication and social media so you can become a social association, or to find out more about Mel's resources, programs and workshops, go to **www.melkettle.com** or email **mel@melkettle.com**.

You can also connect with Mel on social media:

- Twitter – @melkettle
- Instagram – @melkettle
- Facebook – www.facebook.com/MelKettleBiz
- LinkedIn – www.linkedin.com/in/melkettle

Lightning Source UK Ltd.
Milton Keynes UK
UKHW02f1034100718
325485UK00015B/1116/P